RELIGIOUS LIBERTY
IN LATIN AMERICA?

RELIGIOUS LIBERTY

in

LATIN AMERICA?

GEORGE P. HOWARD

Foreword by
JOHN A. MACKAY

PHILADELPHIA

THE WESTMINSTER PRESS

PRINTED IN THE UNITED STATES OF AMERICA

To One Who Has Given Much to South America:

Mae Delvigne Howard,

My Wife

FOREWORD

HERE IS A BOOK THAT DEALS WITH THE GRAVEST SINGLE ISSUE THAT
confronts the Western Hemisphere. Not in our time at least will
this hemisphere be threatened, still less ravaged, by military action
from the side of the Atlantic or the Pacific. But the question arises,
How shall inter-American solidarity be achieved? In what way
can it be secured that mutual understanding and confidence shall
mark relations between American countries? Is it to be seriously
maintained in this country that the propagation of Protestant
Christianity in Latin America, as it has been propagated in North
America, constitutes a hazard and a hurdle to inter-American
comity, even though this propagation be carried on in accordance
with all the laws of propriety and without official sponsorship or
political design? In this volume, representative and authoritative
voices from Latin America make their viewpoints known upon the
subject of relations between the Americas. Never before have the
reasoned opinions of so many eminent Latin-American men and
women been collated upon the particular issue of Protestantism's
status and prestige south of the Rio Grande.

The interpreter of the unique collection of documents that forms
the basis of this book is an Argentine citizen, born of American
parents in the great southern republic, and subsequently educated in the United States. Most of his lifetime has been spent in
Argentina, the land of his birth, or in some other Latin-American
republic. In recent years he has journeyed from one country of
Latin America to another as a Christian apostle to the classes and
masses. In workmen's clubs, in theaters, in university auditoriums,
in Protestant churches, and in the open air, he has interpreted
Christianity and its bearing upon life. Wherever he has gone, he
has been welcomed as a man of spiritual insight and moral passion.

Two years ago, during a visit to the United States, our author,

as he tells us, was startled to find that an insidious movement was
on foot to convince Government circles and the general public —
and especially Church members, both Protestant and Catholic —
that the greatest single obstacle to inter-American comity is the
missionary movement of Evangelical Christianity in the Latin
world. He thereupon undertook a special journey to Latin America. In the course of this journey, he interviewed representative
men and women of different backgrounds and spheres of life,
scarcely one of whom was a Protestant Christian. Jurists, statesmen, men of letters, journalists, diplomats, educators, were in
unanimous agreement that it is utterly untrue to say that Protestant Christianity in Latin America is in any way whatever a stum-
bling block to good will. What they say in effect is this: So far
from the indigenous Protestant Churches of Latin America being a
hindrance to inter-American comity, their work has contributed to
literacy, to the building of moral character, to patriotic loyalty, to
cultural progress, and to community welfare. So far from Protestant missionaries being such an obstacle, many of these men and
women have received signal honors from Governments, as well as
from civic and educational groups. Cranks and misfits there have
been, of course, in the Protestant missionary movement in Latin
America, as in every movement there or elsewhere. But the vast
majority have been the finest interpreters of the spirit and outlook
of the United States that this country has had.

Who is it, then, that have constituted, and continue to constitute, an obstacle to inter-American comity? In Latin America the
centers of difficulty are: feudal barons, Fascist militarists, clerical
politicians, racial absolutists, Nazi and Fascist agents. The feudal
barons have feared contact with liberal labor forces in the United
States. The Fascist militarists have dreamed of the hegemony of
force, and have no use for democratic forms of government. Clerical politicians have promised to conserve the ancient Church in
her agelong status of privilege, in return for the Church's support
of their ambitions. Racial absolutists have aimed to resuscitate the
Colonial era, restore the Spanish Empire, and set everything Hispanic in sharp antagonism to the Anglo-Saxon world. Axis agents
have been interested in creating general pandemonium.

The citizens of the United States who have been an obstacle to inter-American comity have been: unscrupulous men of business, an uncouth and uncultured type of tourist, inept diplomats, and politicians who have not appreciated the Latin temperament or understood Latin America's problems. These matters are set forth in this book with a wealth of vivid illustration and personal anecdote.

But with this we leave Dr. Howard's book and pass on to consider some basic questions suggested by it which are closely related to the whole problem of inter-American relations.

What are the ultimate causes of unrest in the Latin-American world? This is the first basic question. One cause is economic. Poverty is a permanent cause of unrest over a wide area of Latin America. Today, moreover, the growing distress which many of these lands are suffering as a result of the war — whereby food is scarcer, work is more difficult to secure, money has less value — is unhappily becoming associated in the popular mind with the policies of the United States.

There is social unrest. Mexico's social revolution, the first great social revolution of modern times, will eventually spread along the whole Andean chain. This area is in a perpetual state of unstable equilibrium.

There is political unrest. The Spanish Falange, representing Axis forces, is marvelously organized and does its utmost to keep the continent in a ferment and to attribute every evil to the United States. In the shadow of the present demand for national order and stability, due to international conditions, dictators become entrenched in power and increase the volume of underground disquiet.

The chief form of unrest, however, is spiritual in character — spiritual in a broad sense. Hostility to activities of the Roman Catholic Church causes tension throughout the continent. A deep yearning for inner satisfaction and an adequate religious faith moves the souls of millions. In Brazil alone, for example, a cult such as spiritualism is reckoned to have as many as ten million adherents. In cultured circles is heard the anxious query, " Why should the State Department of the U. S. A. appear to relate its policies in Latin America to buttressing the power and prestige of the Roman Catholic Church? " It is insisted that Latin-American countries should not be regarded as a " closed shop," culturally speaking. The demand is also made, in full consonance with the true Latin-American spirit, that all the countries which form the Latin-American group shall be left in perfect freedom, without impositions from any quarter, to select such expressions of human culture as shall appear to them to be desirable to meet their own needs.

There is a second question: *Is it expedient for a democratic government to become the promoter of culture outside the national territory?*

In these last years, the Government of the United States, for the first time in its history, has entered the field of cultural promotion. The totalitarian powers have been past masters at this sort of promotion. Russia, until recently, officially promoted proletarian culture. Germany continues to promote Nazi culture. No democratic government, however, can be a promoter of culture in the same sense that the totalitarian powers can. For in a democracy different cultural heritages are held together, and each is allowed to give itself free expression. The cultural glory of the United States has been its private and independent institutions of learning, and its great state centers of culture, which have not been under Federal control. In this way, the finest kind of cultural equilibrium and freedom has been maintained within the life of the nation.

The moment, however, in which a democratic government undertakes to become the sponsor of culture outside the national territory, it finds itself in immediate danger of following one of the worst trends of the totalitarian powers. When it enters the field of cultural promotion, especially in time of war, it is tempted to make a political criterion determine the aspect of culture to be promoted abroad, as well as the particular agents of culture to be selected for such promotion. In these last years it has come about that the cultural propaganda sponsored by the United States Government in the Americas has given such a position of importance to the Roman Catholic cultural heritage and its representatives that it has, all unintentionally but very decidedly, violated the religious neutrality of the State Department, done a gross injustice to the Protestant heritage of this nation, and played unfair with the best popular opinion in Latin America.

A third question arises: *What is the crucial problem of Latin-American culture?* According to the best and most thoughtful men and women in the Southern continent, it is this: a religious sense of life — that is, a spiritual inwardness, in which religious faith is correlated with moral action and cultural expression. Their complaint is that Latin-American life has lacked a form of spirituality which would give it a sense of wholeness, fullness of meaning, and ethical direction.

The truth is that religion and life have never been closely related in the Latin-American spiritual tradition. Religion has been divorced from culture and ethics by a great unbridged chasm. That chasm, according to representative Latin Americans, has also been the tragedy of Spain. How vehemently have eminent men like Miguel de Unamuno, the Spaniard, and Ricardo Rojas, the Argentinian, indicted the religious tradition of the Spanish and Latin-American people because it has failed to produce true spirituality. Both these great men have given classical formulation to the idea that what Spain and Latin America need more than anything else is a popular and intimate knowledge of the Bible and a reinterpretation of the figure and significance of Jesus Christ. The traditional attitude of the Roman Catholic Church in Spain and Latin America toward the popular reading of the Scriptures has been one of the greatest cultural tragedies in all history.

The fourth question, therefore, is this: *How adequate is Latin-American Catholicism to deal with the cultural situation in the continent which it serves?* The answer is simple. It is utterly unequipped to deal with a problem so difficult and vast.

Up to the present time the record of this Church has been, as North American Catholics know perfectly well, one of the major spiritual derelictions in the history of Christianity. Neither in spiritual resources nor in insight into the true problems of men and nations, nor in the number or prestige of its leaders, can Roman Catholicism in Latin America be looked to for the solution of the

crucial cultural problem of these great countries. Nor can it ever
have the necessary spiritual equipment to do so until Roman Catholic leaders throughout the Iberian world pick up a lost tradition
in Spanish religious history where alone can be found an indigenous fountain of spiritual life. That tradition is discoverable in two
main springs: in the work of the great Spanish mystics whom the
Church persecuted, but who never broke with the Church — Santa
Teresa, John of the Cross, Luís of León; and in the great Spaniards
of the sixteenth century who embraced the principles of Evangelical Christianity, especially the famous laymen Alfonso and Juan
de Valdés. These men are recognized today by authorities on Spanish literature and history as princes of Spanish letters, and peaks
of Spanish moral grandeur. They are, in a word, expressions of the
type of Spanish personality that Evangelical Christianity can produce. Juan de Valdés, more than any other figure in Spanish history, is the true point of departure for the religious reformation
which is needed by the Church in Spain and Latin America.

*How far does the problem of inter-American relations reflect an
internal cultural problem in the United States?* This is the final
question. The United States too has a cultural problem. It has been
passing through a period of cultural atomism. This atomism has
shown itself in the political sphere, as well as in other spheres of
the nation's life and thought. We find it in the ease with which
some Government bureaus have yielded to organized cultural
pressure. The most perfectly organized, and the most politically
minded group, in the modern world is the Roman Catholic hierarchy. Let one calmly think aloud and publicly ask, even at the
risk of being regarded as a bigot, that cognizance be taken of several important facts. The Roman Catholic Church honestly believes that it is the only true Church. It believes, with equal honesty and sincerity, that the ideal political situation is one in which
the true Church alone would be free to propagate its faith, while
the freedom of other forms of religion would be restricted. Members of the latter would enjoy freedom of worship, but would not
be free to carry on religious propaganda. Moreover, the Catholic
hierarchy in the United States now takes the view that there is no
such thing as Protestant solidarity, and that the natural leader of

Christianity in this nation, because of the unity of its organization
and the number of its members, is the Roman Catholic Church.

There are two added circumstances. One doleful fact is this.
As a great living historian recently expressed it, the members of
the Roman Catholic hierarchy in the United States, as distinguished from those in Great Britain, know virtually nothing about
the nature and spirit of Protestant Christianity. The situation of
these hierarchs is totally different from that of the late Cardinal
Hinsley, who was brought up in a Yorkshire rural area, where he
came to understand the glory and strength of the Puritan tradition.
An equally unhappy circumstance is that the Protestant spirit in
the United States, which has done such a splendid job in securing
liberty for every religious group, discourages and even frowns
upon anything that might appear to suggest unworthy or un-
American procedures on the part of any religious group. For this
reason important facts that have emerged in the world of today,
and in the American scene in particular, are rarely spoken about in
public.

Take one illustration of this trend. A book recently published,
entitled *Group Relations and Group Antagonisms*, and edited by
a distinguished American sociologist, R. M. MacIver, takes no
cognizance whatever of the fact that there are Protestant minorities in the world who, in these last years, have suffered brutally at
the hands of the Roman Catholic majority. Why is it necessary to
pass over in silence what has taken place in Spain? Why should
not this able and most valuable book contain an article on Protestant minorities in Spain, in Peru, and in other Roman Catholic
countries in Europe, in Africa, and in America?

For one who knows the Latin-American tradition it is abun-
dantly plain that there is emerging in North American life, in both
the United States and Canada, a new portent. That portent the
people of the Latin world have known for centuries. They have
called it "clericalism," the organized political power of the higher
clergy of the Roman Catholic Church, as distinguished from the
Catholic religious tradition and the mass of the Roman Catholic

people. "Clericalism" has emerged at last in two hospitable Protestant countries in the Western world. Its political pressures and international schemes are becoming perfectly plain. Protestants who have a stainless record of anything that might be regarded as bigotry or intolerance, who will stand for the principle of religious freedom to the last, and will even fight for the rights of Roman Catholics, are now bracing themselves to deal with a new portent in Anglo-Saxon America: the portent, the sinister portent, of Roman Catholic "clericalism." This portent is the source, among other things, of the specious lie that Protestant missions in Latin America are subversive of the Good Neighbor policy.

JOHN A. MACKAY.

Princeton Theological Seminary,
Princeton, N. J.

CONTENTS

INTRODUCTION

I WAS BORN IN ARGENTINA AND HAVE LIVED NEARLY ALL MY LIFE IN South America. I came to the United States in June of 1942 to engage in an extensive program of addresses on Latin America and the Good Neighbor policy. Upon beginning the program which had been outlined, I confronted almost immediately the issue raised by the Roman Catholic campaign against Protestant missionary work in Latin America. This issue could not be dodged. During thirty-five years of active religious and educational work in South America my relations with Roman Catholics have been most friendly and even happy. Some of my firmest support has come from devoted Catholics in that southland who have the intellectual acumen to realize that there are values in Protestantism that greatly benefit their countries. I have always disliked controversy and have not found it necessary in my work in Latin America. But here in the United States I was suddenly face to face with a campaign that was almost as brazen as it was unfair. Statements in the American press so intemperate, even insulting to Protestantism and certainly untrue in many respects, had aroused my audiences and I was compelled to yield to their demand that I answer their questions and meet their interest in this matter.

During a year of constant travel, addressing audiences that have totaled tens of thousands, in colleges and universities, churches and luncheon clubs, speaking sometimes two and three times a day, at Chautauqua, in Florida where eighteen cities were visited, I was impressed with the aroused interest of the American public in this claim of the Roman Catholic hierarchy to religious monopoly in Latin America. I came to this country an " appeaser " of the Roman Catholic Church. I am still a sincere admirer of much that is worthy in that great Church. *But my American audiences drove me out of my irenic position.*

It is difficult to write on these matters without exposing oneself to the charge of bigotry or intolerance. Protestantism has been pushed around a good deal by forces from without that have tried to bluff it and by elements within which are characterized by a timidity unworthy of their heroic tradition. This has led us as Protestants frequently into an attitude of pusillanimity.

A campaign is evidently on for a postwar program that will grant religious freedom wherever the Roman Catholic Church is in a minority and religious monopoly wherever it has the power to suppress competition. The fight against Protestant missions in Latin America is the first stage of that campaign. Our Protestant representatives in the southern lands are the present victims of the bludgeoning blows of misrepresentation and the quick darts of a mocking wit which have been hurled upon them. The discriminatory attitude of the American press in favor of Catholic interests would lead one to plead: If these Catholic interests are allowed to express themselves without the restraints that even pagan courtesy would dictate, surely we Protestants have the right to present our case. Our Roman Catholic friends, therefore, will understand if the writer, after thirty-five years of silence on such delicate matters, feels driven to speak very frankly, but not, he hopes, in a manner that oversteps the bounds of Christian courtesy.

"Whether Protestant missions should be allowed to expand their work in Latin America today, is not a question for us in this country to answer. A reply . . . must come from the people and governments of Latin America," is the pertinent declaration of the Roman Catholic organ, *America,* in an editorial appearing in the issue of December 26, 1942. We thoroughly agree — that is precisely the Protestant position. What do Latin-American Catholics think of the proposed religious segregation of their continent? The aim of this book is to answer that question. It is also important to know what Latin Americans who are not Roman Catholics and who constitute a very considerable part of the population, including so many of the intellectuals, think about the proposed closing of their spiritual frontiers.

Is it true, as critics of Protestant missions allege, that the pres-

ence of American missionaries "is resented throughout the continent [South America] "? Is it true, as one critic says, that " the
South Americans, being innately polite and kind, especially toward foreigners, try to keep up an appearance of courtesy toward
the American missionaries who live among them, but inwardly
their resentment boils like a volcano "? Is it only toward American
missionaries that " resentment boils "?

I have lived all my life among these people; I am one of them;
I was born in South America; but I never discovered any such
general attitude of resentment on the part of the people. Certain
individuals, especially those who fear the common people, who
have no use for democracy, and who hate everything American —
they, of course, " boil like volcanos." And they are not very polite
about it either!

Nevertheless, I began to wonder. Was I mistaken? Had I been
living in a fool's paradise? Was Protestantism hated or resented?
How could this doubt be dispelled? There was only one answer.
I would return to Latin America and interview leaders of thought,
writers, educators, prominent businessmen as well as labor lead-
ers, and ask them candidly and frankly: What do you think of the
Protestants? Are they an obstacle to the Good Neighbor policy?
Should missionaries be recalled?

I thought I would like to recapture some of the experiences that
I had been through in my travels over South America during the
past twenty-five years. I felt that I would like to interview that
Bolivian businessman in La Paz who, not knowing that I was a
Protestant, told me the story of two Indians who had come in
from the Altiplano the day before. " They were clean," he exclaimed. " They were not chewing the coca leaf; they had money.
One bought a sewing machine and the other some bolts of cloth.
They were going to set up a little two-man factory in their village
and make some articles of clothing. When I questioned them I discovered that they belonged to a Protestant mission. They had been
converted, had quit their vices and saved money. *Parece impo-
sible!* It seems impossible! I didn't believe you could do that with
our Indians! " I wonder if that businessman " resented " what the
missions had done for those Indians.

I thought I would drop in to the Ministry of Education in La
Paz and interview the head of the Indian section. I would ask him
what he thought of Peñaranda, Rev. Néstor Peñaranda, if you
please — a full-blooded Indian, the pastor of a Methodist Indian
Church in La Paz, and the cousin of the Bolivian president who
has just been deposed. The Government is using him as one of
the keymen for reaching the Indians culturally. He is a talented
musician; he plays the violin and some of the native Indian instru-
ments, and he sings well. He was sent to Buenos Aires to make
some Indian phonograph records. It was a " damned missionary "
who touched Peñaranda's life when he was a boy, awakening in
him aspirations and hopes which have given Bolivia a man on fire
for his fellow Indians.

I would like to ask the Bolivian Government why they gave
their highest decoration to Dr. Frank D. Beck, American missionary doctor. Was it because they are " deeply offended " at the
presence of missionaries? Beck's story is a fascinating one. Sent
out by the Methodists, he started Ward College in Buenos Aires;
felt the pull of the Indians' tragic need in Bolivia. About that
time he inherited part of a house in the United States. He sold
his part, used the money to go to Chicago University Medical
School, and at great sacrifice he and his wife finished their training, he as a physician and she as a nurse. They returned to Bolivia, established a clinic, and followed the army through the
Chaco war. Then they returned to La Paz where they head a hospital with new buildings and equipment and native trained nurses;
its Christian atmosphere is an honor to the United States and a
glory to Christianity.

I thought that it would be interesting to interview Dr. Antonio Sagarna, member of the Supreme Court of Argentina, who
said recently: " Great Britain has sent many and excellent persons and institutions to the Argentine Republic but her best gift
during the last fifty years was the apostolic personality of William
C. Morris, the most Argentine, the most sacrificial and the most
spiritually fruitful foreigner that I have ever known." [1]

Who was William Morris? A young man who came to Argen-

[1] For complete statement, see Appendix E.

tina as many other young Englishmen have done. But Morris' big
heart was touched by the neglected children of that promising
land and he gave himself with missionary zeal to the cause of education among the poor children of Buenos Aires. When he died a
few years ago he left seven schools, with over six thousand children, and an orphanage, with more than three hundred children.
Most of the money for this marvelous work was given to him by
his Argentine friends and supporters.

So in September of 1943 I left by plane for Chile; from there I
went on to Argentina, Uruguay, and Brazil. Later I was in Bolivia,
Peru, Colombia, and finally Mexico. The majority of the people I
interviewed were Catholics. Several of the countries I visited were
in turmoil with strong dictatorships and many of their leaders
were in concentration camps. My friends said to me: "You could
not have come at a more unpropitious time. These people may be
willing to express their opinions to you privately, but they will be
afraid of being quoted." Nevertheless, I was amazed at the willingness with which they expressed their views. There seemed to
be a feeling on their part that great principles were at stake and
no one should be afraid of declaring his convictions. I was in Colombia during the tense days in which President Alfonso Lopez
left the country and the Liberal party seemed to be balanced on
the edge of a precipice. Every method that the Conservative Catholic party could think of to discredit the liberals was used, including the accusation that they were flooding the country with Protestant missionaries! Could you imagine a more unfavorable
situation in which to ask non-Protestants to declare what they
thought of Protestant missionary work?

The results of my adventurous undertaking will be found in the
succeeding pages of this book. Here are the opinions of some of
the people I interviewed. It would take more than one book to
reproduce all my interviews. Here at least you have a sample.
Here is revealed the fact that there is a strong body of opinion in
Latin America that believes in the work of the Protestants. The
people I interviewed had such strong convictions in favor of religious freedom that they were willing to be quoted and in the
majority of cases they fearlessly signed their names to their state-

ments, people with whom we must reckon in settling the spiritual
problems of our common America.

What is the value of such a compilation of opinions as we here
present? When it comes to estimating how the people of Latin
America feel about Protestant missionaries, there is a wide field
in which anybody can cite selected facts to support his opinion,
whatever it be. There are 120,000,000 people in these southern
republics, and that gives room for a considerable variety of feelings about anything. But it will be a serious error to assume that
the distinguished Latin Americans whose names appear in this
book, most of whom are Roman Catholics, and whose opinions
will be quoted, do not represent a very considerable powerful
body of opinion. No pressure or influence was brought to bear on
them, and the interviewer had in his favor no political or social
prestige. Such ready and courageous response to my questioning is the result of a deep concern and strong convictions regarding the principles and policies which are to prevail in the future
among the peoples of America.

                                                         GEORGE P. HOWARD.

New York City,
May, 1944.

I: Roman Catholics Raise an Issue

THE ROMAN CATHOLIC AGITATION AGAINST PROTESTANT MISSIONS in Latin America was brought out into the open by a manifesto entitled *Victory and Peace,* issued in November of 1942 by Roman Catholic bishops meeting in Washington. It read as follows:

"We send our cordial greetings to our brother Bishops of Latin America. We have been consoled by recent events, which give a sincere promise of a better understanding by our country of the peoples of Mexico, Central and South America.

"Citizens of these countries are bound to us by the closest bond of religion. They are not merely our neighbors; they are brothers professing the same faith. Every effort made to rob them of the Catholic religion or to ridicule it is deeply resented by the peoples of these countries and by American Catholics. These efforts prove to be a disturbing factor in our international relations.

"The traditions, the spirit, the background, the culture of these countries are Catholic. We Bishops are anxious to foster every worthy movement which will strengthen our amicable relations with the republics of this continent.

"We express the hope that the mistakes of the past which were offensive to the dignity of our Southern brothers, their culture and their religion will not continue. A strong bond uniting in true friendship all the countries of the Western Hemisphere will exercise a most potent influence on a shattered post-war world."

Through such periodicals as *The Catholic Digest, Extension,* and *America,* an active campaign was conducted, designed to set the public mind against the idea of Protestant missions in Latin America. Thus the Roman Catholic Church has openly entered the field in an aggressive effort to deprive the Protestant Churches of their right to propagate their faith in the lands to the south.

The gist of the argument is that Latin America is soundly Catholic; that the activities of Protestants there are a "work of pure destruction"; that the presence of missionaries is an obstacle to

1

the Good Neighbor policy; and that they are "the strongest reason why South Americans do not like us." It is alleged that "the great damage done by the American missionaries is in the field of politics. Their work arouses even more enmity against the United States than did the activities of American big business in the old days of dollar diplomacy." *Extension*, the Chicago diocesan paper, in a particularly vituperative editorial said: "There can be no freedom of religion where malevolent interference with the beliefs of Catholic peoples is allowed to run rampant."

These are grave accusations. If true, no one should be more interested in knowing it and acknowledging it than the Protestants. Protestantism makes no claim to "infallibility" and so does not have to save its face by defending its weaknesses. It can admit its blunders and correct its practices. But would it be fair to direct our critical attention only toward the Protestants in Latin America without considering whether the representatives of the Roman Catholic Church have not also made mistakes? In refuting the grave charges brought against the Protestant missionary movement it will be necessary to expose certain facts which Protestants would prefer to ignore. It has been considered by some to be bad form to express one's Protestant convictions which can be stated only in contrast with Catholic doctrines and attitudes. A false conception of the spirit of Christian charity has been invoked. One cannot but admire the straight-out-from-the-shoulder attitude of Catholic writers. Take this paragraph, for instance, from an address by Msgr. John P. Treacy, of Cleveland, Ohio, to the Catholic Daughters of America convened in Washington, D. C., during July, 1943, and published in *The Evening Star* (July 14):

"The American Protestant churches exported missionaries into Latin America to convert the natives who were 100 per cent Catholic whether they practiced their religion or not. These people wanted their one true faith or no religion and the United States had little or no faith to offer and about 200 so-called religions. Naturally these people resented the colonists from the United States."

This is plain talk. There is no mincing of words here, no false sentimentalism. We know where Msgr. Treacy stands. I cannot believe that when he says that "the United States had little or no faith to offer and about 200 so-called religions" to export, he was representing the best and most enlightened Roman Catholic opinion in America. But he does represent a most aggressive pressure group within that Church and a group that enjoys much power and favor at present in Washington. To stand up and answer that sort of verbiage would not be the answer of bigotry or intolerance or vulgar suspicion. On the contrary it would be an answer based on tolerance. It would be an answer in thorough harmony with good will and a sense of fair play.

The Roman Catholic Church has the right to believe that no one is saved outside of her communion. Protestants concede to Catholics the right of propaganda as they cherish it for themselves. But when Catholics ask the American Government to refuse permission to new Protestant missionaries to go to Latin America or to those on furlough to return to their long-established home and work on the southern continent, then they are claiming the right of persecution. Will the people of the United States approve of their State Department's deciding whether properly qualified Protestant missionaries shall be sent to carry on their missionary work in the countries to the south of us?

Roman Catholic emissaries to South America move freely, while passports for Protestant missionaries are hard to get. The necessity for restricting travel on account of war conditions is not the reason why the State Department discriminates against Protestant missionaries. That difficulty exists and is recognized by the Protestant mission boards, who have been parsimonious in their requests for passports.

Nor does the difficulty lie primarily with the South American Governments. With two or three exceptions, countries where military dictatorships keep themselves in power against popular will by the support of the Roman Catholic hierarchy, there are no more restrictions on entrance into those countries than are natural during wartimes. Evidently the State Department believes that the approach to Latin America must be through Roman Catholicism. Ambassadors and consular agents in increasing numbers are Roman Catholics or followers of Roman Catholic policy. One of

the most distinguished cultural attachés sent to South America, a
well-known scientist and a worthy representative of the cultural
life of the United States, was received by the ambassador under
whom he was to serve, himself a notorious non-Churchman, with
this rebuff: "I want you to know that I was opposed to your appointment because you are not a Catholic."

The Department of State, especially during the present war
conditions, has a perfect right to inquire if Americans wishing to
go abroad are going for subversive or immoral purposes. But it is
hard to see what right it has to pass on the religious qualifications
or affiliations of an American citizen who asks for a passport. It is
even more difficult not to sympathize with the Protestants when
they ask that the Christian missionary enterprise be considered
just as legitimate as the business of exporting American ciga-
rettes, cars, books, or drugs, and that it be considered at least as
important as sending health missionaries to South America under
the Rockefeller Foundation, or financial missionaries under Dr.
Kemmerer, or engineering missionaries to build up a steel industry in Brazil.

Latin Americans coming to the United States are kept within
Roman Catholic auspices. In his interviews with South Americans
who had come to the United States, in most cases as guests
of honor of the American Government, the writer constantly
discovered perplexity and even resentment created in the minds
of these distinguished visitors by this policy of the State Department.

The president of the São Paulo, Brazil, National University,
Dr. Jorge Americano, commented on this strange tendency of the
State Department. Dr. Americano is a Roman Catholic and one of
Brazil's outstanding lawyers and educators.

"I noticed something curious when I went to the United States
recently with my family," he said to me. "Everybody who had
any official contact with me was an American Catholic."

"Do you think that is wise?" I immediately asked him. "Do
you think it necessary?"

"Not at all," he answered; "an educated person can get along
on good terms with Catholics or Protestants. A cultured Brazilian

would never dream of asking whether the person who was show-
ing him some attention was a Catholic or a Protestant. In dealing
with others the important thing is to be urbane, tactful, and gen-
tlemanly."

Dr. Gil Salgueiro, of Uruguay, was invited to lecture in the
United States; he is not a Roman Catholic and has been nurtured
in the anticlerical tradition which is particularly strong in Uruguay. Yet he was sent to lecture exclusively in Roman Catholic
institutions of the United States. A former Uruguayan minister of
education, whose name I shall omit, was invited by the American
Government to come to the United States in 1943. When I interviewed him recently in Montevideo, he said to me: "On my first
Sunday in Washington I asked what there was to see and do in
that city on Sunday. They gave me the address of a famous Roman Catholic Church! And I, who would not be seen entering a
Catholic Church in Uruguay, took the suggestion and went to
Church! I was surprised to see how many people attended mass.
In fact, I was impressed with the large crowds that attend Church
in the United States. I noticed that everyone seemed to have the
idea that because we came from South America we were all Roman Catholics. Five prominent Uruguayan newspaper editors
were invited to the United States; only one of the five was a Roman Catholic and he was the editor of the Catholic daily, *El Bien
Publico*. At a reception given in my honor by a Pan-American
organization in San Francisco there were fifteen people present
of whom six were Roman Catholic priests."

It is tragic that liberal Roman Catholics and Government officials in the United States should not have realized before this how
repugnant this policy of "religious segregation" or the "closed
door" is to the average South American, even to those who are
Roman Catholics. For the people of South America lived during
three hundred years in a closed and isolated continent and the
original impulse of the fight for independence came not so much
from a desire to be separated from Spain as from the irresistible
will to be in free contact with the rest of the world. South Americans know what it is to be "protected" from outside and so-called
dangerous ideas or relationships. The reaction against this policy

of paternalistic manipulation has swung them fiercely toward the opposite tendency of an almost passionate cult of freedom.

Hence the rise of anticlericalism in Spanish America. That term means little or nothing to the average American unless it be to imply something discreditable. "Clericalism" is the priest stepping out of his high function as a representative of spiritual values and using religion itself for the worldly ends of the Church. South America knows it well and has suffered under its handicap for centuries. On that continent will be found many anticlericals who are good Roman Catholics. In a copy of a leading daily published in Bogotá, Colombia, and which I have before me, Dr. Armando Solano, a great liberal and sincere Catholic, says: "Popular belief in and support of a creed may be weakened not only as a result of anti-religious propaganda, which I dislike immensely, but also as a consequence of the anti-national and unwise attitudes of the clergy. I think that it is possible to be a Catholic and at the same time be anticlerical."

On his return from a visit to the United States in 1941, Manuel Seoane, editor of Chile's most popular weekly, *Ercilla*, gave his impressions of the United States in a book which is instructive reading, *El Gran Vecino* [2] (*The Big Neighbor*). Seoane was born in Peru, but because of his liberal and democratic leanings and his qualities of leadership he was expatriated by the dictatorships of his country. He is a Roman Catholic and one of his sisters is a nun in a teaching order in the United States. In his book he mentions the fact that on the ship that brought him to the United States several Protestant missionaries were returning to their native land. He remarks: "They went out to preach their Gospel in an atmosphere that was narrow and hostile. Now the Protestant pastors return while Catholic priests go out by the dozens. It is the new policy (of the American government) of leaning upon the Catholic Church in its dealing with certain Indo-American countries. Catholicism in the United States is a solid and homogeneous force. Roosevelt had to yield to its powerful influence during the Spanish civil war. As a Church it carries much influence and represents many votes. Now the foreign policy, as regards our con-

[2] Edit. Orbe, Santiago, Chile, 1943.

tinent, lays its snares through the medium of Papal missionaries." [3]

South Americans are remarkably aware and suspicious of what Señor Seoane calls the "directed religious policy" of the State Department. In a written statement (see Appendix A) he says:

". . . We are witnessing a 'directed religious policy' which requires that the abundant flow of American functionaries to South America should fulfill, if possible, the prerequisite of being Roman Catholic.

"We Latin Americans are inclined to be distrustful. We ask ourselves: Why does a country which is predominantly Protestant send us delegations that are predominantly Catholic? Why does it try to hide its Protestantism?

"The labor groups in Latin America are also keenly aware of this problem. At a recent convention of the Chilean Confederation Workers, which controls 500,000 members, three American delegates came from the United States. They were all Catholics. Consternation was created when these delegates visited a small Roman Catholic labor organization and were reported to have said, 'Catholic workingmen must prepare to take under their control the direction of the labor movement.' This declaration alarmed the Chilean labor delegates. They are determined not to allow clerical influences to penetrate their organization.

"This attitude of favoring everything that is Roman Catholic has gone to the extreme of making it difficult for Protestant missionaries to travel to South America. This is a very serious matter. Among us freedom of religion is established by our constitutions and it offends us to think that an inquisitorial office has been established in some passport department which decides to whom we are to extend our hospitality! We want the best North Americans to come to our shores, be they Catholic or Protestant. The only requirement is that they should come with an authentic spirit of good neighborliness, desirous of fostering a progressive understanding and friendship between these two portions of the New World."

I almost literally sat at the feet of one of Peru's really great men, whose name I shall omit for obvious reasons. Living rather qui-

[3] *Ibid.*, p. 28.

etly, almost in retirement — South American dictatorships have no place for men of genius or originality — he has had enough honors heaped upon him in other years to more than compensate him for the ingratitude of the present governing oligarchy. He has a distinguished record in diplomacy to his credit, and the Spanish-speaking world long ago acclaimed him as one of its brilliant literary lights.

"Is the present American ambassador a Roman Catholic?" he asked. That was in 1943; I said that he was not.

"Well, he favors everything Roman Catholic," was his answer. "Most of the exchange students chosen to go to the United States are Roman Catholic. So are the professors. Many of these are out-and-out Fascists. And they have come back from the United States more confirmed in their Fascism. I have heard them say: Democracy is a myth in the United States. There is the same attitude in that country toward race that the Fascists have. Others have said: If the democracies win, 'American imperialism' will be more dangerous than ever, for the United States will come out of the war a mighty military power.

"The liberals don't talk this way," he explained; "only the conservatives. 'The United States is meddling in everything,' say these conservatives. 'They distribute newsprint; they are the providers of many things we need; they have even helped to keep certain books out of Peru.' Many of these Conservative Catholics who work in harmony with the co-ordinator's office are using this relation to keep themselves in power politically."

One of Argentina's busiest and most dynamic men is Dr. Américo Ghioldi, member of the Argentine Congress, an authority on educational matters and editor of the influential Buenos Aires daily, *La Vanguardia*. During 1942 he came to the United States as a member of a commission appointed by the Argentine Government to study some aspects of the American school system. As I write, word comes that *La Vanguardia* has made the drastic decision of interrupting its faithful record of forty years and refuses to appear under the restrictions imposed by the Argentine Government upon the press. It is the only paper, so far, that has had the courage to go on "strike" against the dictatorship.

"For many South Americans," said Dr. Ghioldi to me, "the attitude of the United States in strengthening political power of the Catholic Church in South America, especially in those countries in which that Church adheres to the autocratic forms of government, is viewed with alarm. The final result is the strengthening of dictatorship on our continent.

"I am not hostile towards Catholicism. But it is necessary to emphasize that in Latin America there is a predominance of a clergy which has been educated in the Hispanic and Roman tradition whose spirit differs so fundamentally from that of militant Catholicism in other parts.

"North American public opinion must understand that the Good Neighbor policy means concretely that the Atlantic Charter must also hold good for these parts of the world where there is much official talk of democracy and liberty but where people still live in subjugation." [4]

It was a red-letter day when I was ushered into the private study of Dr. Hugo Fernandez Artucio, a distinguished lawyer, member of the Uruguayan Legislature, university professor, and member of "The Free World Association." Dr. Artucio became famous three years ago when he exposed the Nazi spy system in South America. He is the author of *The Nazi Underground in South America*.[5] He was invited to this country by the United States Government as an official guest and as a recognition of his services to the cause of the United Nations. Here is a quotation from a statement written after his return:

"The influence of Catholic intolerance reflected in the foreign policy of the United States is considered by people of liberal spirit in this country as a dangerous symptom of the totalitarian leanings of the United States. Therefore, there is a feeling of resentment among liberal sections of Uruguayan public opinion because of this surprising aspect of American policy. The problem is world-wide. Marshal Petain, influenced by the worst Catholic elements in France, repudiated the democratic principles of the French Revolution. Admiral Leahy, and later Mr. Murphy, seemed

[4] For complete statement, see Appendix B.
[5] Farrar, 1942.

able to accommodate themselves very easily to this attitude which means at the same time a repudiation of the Bill of Rights of the United States. This anti-American policy which the representatives of the United States look upon with indifference if not approval, affects the fundamental ethics of inter-American relations. The influence of Ambassador Hayes (a Catholic) in Spain has always been in the direction of favoring the totalitarianism of Franco. It is believed that the special representative to the Vatican, Mr. Taylor, has helped in determining all the subsequent policy in North Africa and in Italy. Similar examples could be given with respect to Czecho-Slovakia, Hungary, etc.

"I have lived for two years in the United States and I hold a deep affection for its people. The foundation of democracy in that country is the small community of Puritan tradition. Evidently there is a clerical revolution underway in the world to destroy the gains which up to the present have been made for democracy. This is especially dangerous in the United States. I have heard complaints that the Government of the United States often sends people to these republics who are Roman Catholics and who are inclined with a sectarian spirit to favor everything that is Catholic. Unfortunately, this brings to life again among us a problem which we had thought was solved once for all; at least as far as Uruguay was concerned." [6]

There are other aspects of this problem which do not seem to have occupied the attention of Roman Catholics in the United States and members of the State Department who believe that the elimination of foreign missionaries in South America would strengthen the Good Neighbor policy.

What are you going to do with the British foreign missionaries, the German, Dutch, Norwegian, Armenian, and French Protestant missionaries? At least 40 per cent of the foreign Protestant religious workers in Latin America are from European countries. Our State Department could do nothing about them. Of the 471 foreign missionaries (Anglicans, Americans, Norwegians, et cetera) listed in an official directory of missionary activity in Argentina and Uruguay, only 140 are North Americans. And this number in-

[6] For complete statement, see Appendix C.

cludes the wives of missionaries. This is for a territory larger than the entire United States east of the Mississippi!

Then again, would the Roman Catholic Church in South America be rid of all religious rivals if the foreign missionaries were withdrawn? Not at all. Protestantism in Latin America is no longer an exotic minority; it has become an indigenous movement that is very largely self-governing and self-propagating. In Chile the largest Protestant group is that of the Pentecostals, who number 30,-000 and among whom there is not a single foreign missionary. Their pastors are Chilean. In Uruguay and Argentina, which together constitute what the Methodists call an "Annual Conference," this governing body has a native-born bishop, seventy-six national (or native) workers and pastors, and only four foreign missionaries. What would be achieved by withdrawing these four missionaries? In Uruguay the strong Waldensian Church is entirely autonomous and has no foreign missionaries. The same is true of the Peruvian Evangelical Church. In Brazil there are two independent and completely autonomous Churches: the Congregational and an Independent Presbyterian organization. It can also be said of the Methodist Church in Brazil that it is independent and autonomous. It elects its own bishops and determines its own program and policies.

Furthermore, it must be remembered that the American or foreign missionary is, with rare exceptions, a restraining influence in all contacts or controversy with the Roman Catholic Church. Withdraw the American missionary and you will immediately set free the unrestrained feelings of Spaniards, Italians, and native South Americans, many of whom came out of Romanism with bitter memories and no training in the control of invective. An anti-Catholic pamphlet of very violent language, which had circulated in Colombia and had stirred up great resentment among the Catholics as well as criticism from American diplomatic representatives, was found to have been written by a Spanish ex-priest. No responsible Protestant group had ever used it, and at a meeting of missionaries representing several boards it was unanimously condemned.

At a Eucharistic Congress held in Cali, Colombia, a Protestant

created a considerable stir by distributing a leaflet criticizing the
Roman Catholic interpretation of the Eucharist. On investigation
it was found that the distributor of this leaflet was himself a Colombian, who had at his own expense printed the offending leaflet and ignored the pleas of his American missionary pastor that
he should not molest the Catholics in their celebration. What is to
be done with this national or native opposition to Romanism?
The removal of missionaries, trained in what some might consider
the excessive spirit of tolerance which is characteristic of Great
Britain and America, would inexorably release an avalanche of
aggressive controversy that would greatly embitter relations between Protestants and Catholics in Latin America.

Protestantism does not fear competition. True religion, it believes, is too strong to be shaken by the attack of atheists, the scof-
fing doubts of unbelievers, or the opposition of some rival faith.
True religion needs no legal protection. If the Roman Catholic
Church can influence the moral and spiritual life of Latin America
so vitally as to win the people of those lands back to its faith,
well and good. If it can win ours from us, so be it. But we shall
not stand by if it attempts to do all this by invoking Government
protection. We shall honor it if it gains these ends by the method
of persuasive appeal, by the example of a priesthood more " exemplary " than our missionaries, and by the skill of a faith that
reasons more cogently and thinks more deeply.

The American people should be deeply concerned over this
whole matter of religious liberty in the light of possible postwar
policies. Ethiopia was not a Roman Catholic country, and yet
when it was conquered by Italy it became a preserve for missionaries of that Church. Several Protestant Scandinavian missionaries
were driven out of the country, as well as the Presbyterians who,
with school and hospital, had been rendering altruistic service.
Franco has annihilated Protestantism in Spain, and is hailed by
the Vatican as " the saviour of Christianity."

This is not just another quarrel between the Churches. There
are precious principles at stake. Lovers of freedom dare not keep
silent. Americans want freedom for every person to worship God
in his own way everywhere in the world. This is the freedom for

which the founding fathers came to America. And they built so well that their concept of freedom widened and soon they were not only claiming it for themselves but offering it to others. It would indeed be tragic if today of all days, when we are in a war to defend the "four freedoms," we should surrender this deeper freedom without which none of the other freedoms can stand.

This is a day which calls for the utmost unity among the freedom-loving peoples of the world. This is not a time to seek sectarian advantage at the cost of such unity. The democracy for which free men are fighting around the world must not be sabotaged for the advantage of any particular body.

This matter has its bearing, not only upon Latin America, but perhaps even more seriously on what might occur in the United States. As Dr. H. P. Van Dusen pointed out in *Christianity and Crisis* (January 11, 1943): "Those whose memories reclaim the bitter years following the last war cannot forget the whirlwinds of intolerance which swept across the nation, the resurgence of the Ku Klux Klan, the passions of persecution against minority groups, racial, economic and religious. Signs are not lacking that the same madness may have to be combatted in the coming aftermath. If that day comes, Protestants will wish to rally to the defense of Catholic liberties as well as their own. But it will not be easy if Catholic leaders have sought to rob minority groups in South America of the very rights which they, a minority group, so freely enjoy in North America."

The Roman Catholic bishops in the United States have issued recently a warning on the occasion of the Moscow agreement that "religious liberty as we understand it in the United States is non-existent in Russia." That's true. But it is also true that religious liberty as we understand it is nonexistent in every country that is predominantly Roman Catholic: Spain, Portugal, Italy, Poland, and Peru. The Catholic bishops and press do well to demand the maximum of religious liberty in the world after the war. It is to be hoped that they will agree that their splendid stand on religious liberty should apply also to Catholic countries.

Back of this whole question of Protestant missions in " Catholic " countries lies the much deeper question of the nature of religious liberty. In such a world as free men are trying to build, should it be accepted as a principle that the religion of every area must be frozen as it was at some earlier date? Such a policy cannot be defended. The Roman Catholic Church herself does not accept it, for while she advocates the closed door for Latin America, Spain, and Italy, she wants no sacred monopoly recognized in India for Hinduism, in China for Buddhism, or in England and the United States for Protestantism.

What attitude are American Catholics going to take regarding the proposal to combine the gospel of the four freedoms with the doctrine of a closed continent for Catholics? One good result of this current controversy is that it is forcing us to re-examine what we mean by religious liberty.

II : The Issue of Religious Liberty

IN THE *THE FOUR FREEDOMS*, A PAMPHLET ISSUED BY AN AGENCY OF the United States Government, the following appears in the section on " Freedom of Religion ": " The democratic guarantee of freedom of worship is not in the nature of a grant — it is in the nature of an admission. It is the state admitting that the spirit soars in illimitable regions beyond the collectors of customs. It was Tom Paine, one of the great voices of freedom in early America, who pointed out that a government could no more grant to man the liberty of worshiping God than it could grant to God the liberty of receiving such worship."

This is precisely the Protestant position.

The well-known Spanish writer, Salvador de Madariaga, in a recent radio broadcast from London, discusses the freedom of man. He said that man was given his freedom by God himself. " But," asks Madariaga, " man is free for what? To follow or proclaim error? Yes. Because only as error is freely expressed will it see itself the object of an equally free critical attack. . . . Freedom of thought is a guarantee of social peace."

That also is the Protestant position.

In view of the significance of this whole question, the reply of the Federal Council of Churches [7] to the pronouncement of the Roman Catholic hierarchy against Protestant missions in Latin America was very timely:

" We deplore the pretension of the Roman Catholic hierarchy to circumscribe the religious freedom of Protestant Christians in the proclamation of their faith, while by implication reserving for themselves the right to universal proclamation of their own. We can imagine no policy more certain to project into the New World the baneful intolerance which is now producing such tragic consequences in the contemporary life of Spain."

[7] See statement, *Our Heritage of Freedom,* issued at its annual meeting held in Cleveland, Ohio, December, 1942.

No more satisfactory statement of the Protestant theory of religious freedom could be found than that which was issued in March of 1944 by the Joint Committee on Religious Liberty of the Federal Council of Churches:

"We recognize the dignity of the human person as the image of God. We therefore urge that the civic rights which derive from that dignity be set forth in the agreements into which our country may enter looking toward the promotion of world order, and be vindicated in treaty arrangements and in the functions and responsibilities assigned to international organizations. States should assure their citizens freedom from compulsion and discrimination in matters of religion. This and the other rights which inhere in man's dignity must be adequately guarded; for when they are impaired, all liberty is jeopardized.

"The right of individuals everywhere to religious liberty shall be recognized and, subject only to the maintenance of public order and security, shall be guaranteed against legal provisions and administrative acts which would impose political, economic, or social disabilities on grounds of religion.

"Religious liberty shall be interpreted to include freedom to worship according to conscience and to bring up children in the faith of their parents; freedom for the individual to change his religion; freedom to preach, educate, publish, and carry on missionary activities; and freedom to organize with others, and to acquire and hold property, for these purposes.

"To safeguard public order and to promote the well-being of the community, both the state, in providing for religious liberty, and the people, in exercising the rights thus recognized, must fulfil reciprocal obligations. The state must guard all groups, both minority and majority, against legal disabilities on account of religious belief; the people must exercise their rights with a sense of responsibility and with charitable consideration for the rights of others."

An article on the Roman Catholic conception of religious liberty [8] written by Father W. Eugene Shiels, associate editor of

[8] *America*, January 23, 1943.

America, a Jesuit periodical, seems to express agreement with the Protestant position on religious freedom:

" Every man has the right by nature (and not by some grant of government) to follow his conscience, that is, to serve God as he sees God wants to be served. He must try to find the true religion. He must follow the light as God gives him to see it. He has the duty, and the right, so to act. He must follow his conscience, whether correct or erroneous, though certainly if he sees it to be in error he is obliged to seek a way out of the error to the truth. This right to follow conscience comes from the duty to do the very same thing. That is why we have the right, so that we may perform the duty.

" Religion includes three essential acts: belief, worship, and moral conduct in accordance with that belief and worship. And the irreducible minimum of protection for this freedom requires that a man be allowed to hold the beliefs, perform the worship, and keep to the code of morals given him by his Maker. Anything less than this is absolute tyranny and could not be tolerated in a treaty of world peace. No government would in this matter have the right to tell other governments to mind their own business and leave it to its own concerns. It simply has not any just power to deny this minimum to a human being."

This is highly satisfactory as far as it goes, though it presents a strange contrast to the Roman Catholic demands that religious liberty for Protestants should be restricted in South America. Will the Roman Catholic Church henceforth accord full religious liberty to Protestants in countries where it claims dominance? Not at all. For as we read on we discover that the joker lies in distinguishing between " religious liberty " and " religious activity."

" Religious liberty is one thing," says Father Shiels; " broad religious activity quite another. Every state must preserve the true religion, so, too, every state must respect the right of religious liberty. But not every state must allow the broadest religious activity."

Doubts are immediately aroused by the use of the term " the true religion." Who is to decide what is the true religion? To the

Roman Catholic Church "the true religion" does not mean the religion which a man's conscience, aided by the Holy Scriptures and guided by the Holy Spirit, accepts. It means the Roman Catholic religion.

"Suppose that some country," continues Father Shiels, "having a quite uniform religious picture, admits immigrants of another religion. Must it give the immigrant group the fullest privileges in propagating its cult? Not unless that group can demonstrate, to the conviction of the state, a special divine mandate to carry on its activity."

But would it ever be possible to demonstrate a special divine mandate on terms that would be acceptable to a state dominated by a hierarchy that applies such qualifications to its definition of religious liberty? We doubt it. Under such a theory of religious freedom no minority group need ever expect "the fullest privileges in propagating its cult."

The application of this theory of forcibly limiting the religious function of minorities in countries where nearly everyone professes the same religion would keep Christian missionaries out of all non-Christian lands and would have kept Roman Catholicism out of the United States.

A French Catholic writer, Louis Veuillot, has summed up the official attitude of the Church regarding the rights of minorities, in these words: [9] "When we are in a minority, we ask for religious liberty in the name of your (Protestant) principles. When we are in a majority, we refuse it in the name of ours."

Leo XIII, in his encyclical *On the Christian Constitution of States*, points out the "deficiencies" of some democracies. He enumerates (1) their failure to "make public profession of religion, and that the true one"; (2) the fact that "the Catholic religion is allowed a standing in civil society equal only" to that of others; and (3) the evil of granting freedom of speech and publication. Msgr. John A. Ryan, director of the social action department of the National Catholic Welfare Conference, in his *Catho-*

---

[9] Quoted in article "Freedom as Interpreted by Rome," by A. Stewart McNairn, in *World Dominion and the World Today*. London, July–August, 1943.

lic Principles of Politics (1940), referring to this encyclical and defending the desirability of limiting the liberty of non-Catholics in a Catholic country, says: " Superficial champions of religious liberty will promptly and indignantly denounce the foregoing propositions as the essence of intolerance. They are intolerant, but not therefore unreasonable. Error has not the same rights as truth. Since the profession and practice of error are contrary to human welfare, how can error have rights? How can the voluntary toleration of error be justified? " But would the American people consider as democratic a regime in which there is no toleration of anything that the Roman Catholic hierarchy calls error?

The natural reaction to all this is the conviction that the Roman Catholic Church does not interpret religious liberty as the democratic world understands it.

In spite of the fact that millions of our men are today fighting for the four freedoms, one of which is freedom of religion, not as Msgr. Ryan and the Roman Catholic hierarchy authoritatively define it, but as it is commonly understood by American citizens, will the Roman Catholic Church persist in its attempt to drive the Protestant minority out of Latin America? We are opposed to the policy of an authoritative religious dictatorship for that or any other continent. In things of the spirit as in things material, the principle of monopoly has had and will continue to have most unhappy results. The Christian Churches are being challenged to close their ranks and unite their forces for postwar reconstruction. But it is obvious that it will not be possible to rehabilitate the twentieth century with thirteenth-century ideas.

An editorial in the May, 1944, number of the Bulletin published by the Federal Council of Churches representing twenty-five Protestant denominations accepts the principle that American Government representatives, in their relations with other peoples, should stand as the unashamed exponents of certain ideals which have been, from the beginning, in the very life stream of the United States. " There may be frequent occasions," it says, " during the next few years when our Church people will be called upon to remind the government [of the U. S.] of the necessity of vindicating our national policy (in regard to religious liberty) in so far as possible in dealing with other nations. We recognize that our government cannot impose American policy upon other countries; but we believe it appropriate that our national influence in the world community should strengthen the forces of democracy, which requires the recognition of the rights and obligations of religious liberty."

When the Roman Catholic hierarchy of Peru, by means of a last-minute strategy, seemed about to prevent the holding of a Protestant youth conference in the capital of that country in 1942, with delegates from every Latin-American country as well as the United States, an appeal was made to the Argentine, Uruguayan, Mexican, Chilean, and Bolivian ambassadors to use their friendly offices so that this purely religious assembly, whose delegates were already on the way, might be allowed to convene. There was the most gratifying willingness on the part of these distinguished South Americans to help in any way that was possible. It was with shame that some of us discovered the deep-seated conviction of the members of the organizing committee of Peruvian youth that it would be futile to ask for counsel or help in that crisis from the diplomatic representatives of the United States.

A Protestant bishop asked permission in August of 1943 to enter a certain South American country for the purpose of visiting the Churches and schools of his denomination. It was refused by the Foreign Minister, who is notoriously bigoted and antidemocratic. The bishop happened to be a South American and a citizen of Uruguay. When the Uruguayan ambassador, who is not a Protestant, learned of the incident, he immediately called on the Foreign Minister.

" Your Excellency," he said, " I have come to ask why you have refused admission to this Uruguayan citizen."

" He is a Protestant and we do not want such people to enter our country," was the answer.

" I know nothing about that," parried the ambassador. " He is a citizen of my country and held there in high esteem. Why is he not admitted? "

The bishop was admitted, but this and other unconstitutional acts of the small, reactionary group represented by this minister finally aroused the congress of that country. They reminded the minister that the constitution of their country guaranteed freedom of religion and that neither he nor anyone else had any legal right to exclude anyone from entrance into the country on religious grounds. Instructions have since been sent to all the consular agents of that country, instructing them that on no account are the religious affiliations of applicants to be used as a reason for refusing passport visas.

Every one of the twenty Latin-American countries has written into its constitution a clause guaranteeing freedom of religion. Of the twenty, eleven have separation of Church and State. The South American people are proud of this liberalism and they deeply resent the machinations of reactionary minorities who, in some of the republics, are trying to turn back the wheels of progress.

And if the policy of expediency leads the United States of America and Great Britain to silence their testimony on behalf of a right which is at the very roots of their national life, voices will be raised and are being raised on behalf of religious freedom in Latin America, voices that no dictator or reactionary group or appeasing political realism will be able to silence.

One such voice is that of Gabriela Mistral, the Chilean poetess and writer, loved and honored all over Latin America. The pride of the Chilean Government and people in this distinguished woman took tangible form in her appointment as Chilean Consul General at Large. She moves from country to country as an ambassador of the things of the spirit. She is a Roman Catholic, and on the question of religious liberty she gave me the following statement: [10]

" Freedom for all creeds is one of the distinguishing republican honors of South America. The laws which establish that freedom are a guarantee, first of all, for the Catholics, then for the Protestants, and also for the Orthodox Church and the Jews. Tampering with that pillar of bronze, which is our religious liberty, hammered out for us on a thrice heated forge, or mutilating the

[10] For complete statement, see Appendix H.

struggling roots of the spirit of freedom, seems an adventure
fraught with danger, and I always fear such ventures on the part
of young and inexperienced peoples. Such enterprises stir up, first
of all, curious fancies, then release dark passions and finally lend
strength to evil instincts.

" I am not foigetting the position of Catholicism in Latin America. It is the highest in the plane of our moral institutions. Numerically her strength is overwhelming and by her side others are
like weak reeds or tender saplings. Lords and masters well established in their broad moral domains, the Catholicisms of the south,
and the Chilean leading them all, permitted themselves the luxury of being generous, — a grace always elegant, and they consented to live together with other creeds and sects. The laws that
separate Church and State, accepted in Chile by the *sagesse* of a
prince of the Church who was also princely in his wisdom, Msgr.
Errázuriz, do not signify the surrender of the Catholic conscience
to the State. Some of us believe they mean something very different. We believe they signify a degree of liberation that leads to
greater ease and comfort. Nearly all States tend to overwhelm the
representatives of spiritual values, belittling them with a protection that carries with it the suspicion of some deal or barter.

" On the other hand, the proposition that Protestantism should
be sacrificed could turn out to be a Trojan horse to Catholicism.
To begin with, as far as I know, it has not been suggested by
South American Roman Catholicism.

" Supposing that Protestant missions and their social service activities could be suppressed, either rapidly or gradually, I fear
that, little by little, an atmosphere of resentment and finally of
hatred for Catholicism would be engendered.

" I am filled with doubt and even fear at the thought of a Catholic domination based on eliminations or on restrictions double-
dyed in privilege. Creeds, just as with strong government regimes,
do not need the support of favor or privilege. And if they seek
such favors or accept them, they fall into great temptation."

" What other reasons would you mention that justify the continuation of Protestant work in Spanish America? " was one of my
final questions to Gabriela Mistral.

"The primary reason, which should have been mentioned sooner, is that those activities fall within what the League of Nations calls the 'rights of minorities.' A careful census of Protestants in our midst would reveal an impressive total. To weaken or suppress their institutions would be in the nature of an odious illegality. It would lead to a resentment and later to dangerous outbursts. It is outstandingly true that liberty alone conciliates, placates and calms.

"We Iberian Catholics must remember that these Anglo-Saxon and South American Protestant groups need their churches, their services of worship, and their religious press just as much as they need the piece of ground on which they have built their homes, their factories and their playgrounds. They feed equally upon the food of our soil, the teaching of their religious books and the word of their missionaries. And this spiritual hunger seems to me to be more intense in them than in us. I have not seen our people carrying the Gospels in the minimum baggage allowed for a plane trip. I have seen your Protestant people do that. Life in these lands of ours, to be happy, must be complete. No Christian can consider life fulfilled, if it lacks the salt of high wisdom. Protestants are entitled to their share of spiritual teaching just as they receive their portion of grain and native fruits."

Dr. Alberto Casal Castel is a well-known Argentine educator and Government inspector of secondary education. He is an active Roman Catholic and the only layman who writes on religious subjects for the Argentine press. Among other questions, I put the following to him: "What importance do you attach to the principle of religious liberty?" And he answered: [11]

"I was born in a country (Argentina) that practices freedom of worship, because it is a country made up of a population of immigrant origin. I have been nurtured in the liberal ideas which through the influence of John B. Alberdi were incorporated in our political Constitution. Thus our land could 'appeal to all men everywhere who desire to live on Argentine soil.' Consequently I cannot help but be in favor of religious tolerance. Besides this we need men whose lives are organized around a certain type of faith

[11] For this complete statement, see Appendix D.

and whose morality would spring from that faith. This is very important, as I see it, and much more beneficial than a flow of individuals to our country with no faith at all. They could offer us no moral security for the future."

"Does religious liberty consist only in freedom to worship God according to one's conscience or does it also include the right of propaganda in favor of one's beliefs?" I next asked him.

"Freedom must be interpreted in the broadest possible way. It must be understood as the autonomy of the conscience and as carrying with it the right of propaganda. Liberty is not an accident in the Christian life but rather its essential condition, it is the *sine qua non* of Christianity. Without freedom we cannot live out our doctrine, we cannot even understand it. Liberty is so fundamental that I insist that it is also the right of those who do not believe as we do. We should not deprive others of that which we would not want them to deprive us. In the measure to which we respect the freedom of others, ours will be preserved."

In his letter to me enclosing these answers Dr. Casal Castel says: "I belong to the fraternity of world Christians. And I am grateful to you for the opportunity which you have conferred upon me of having my convictions reach the United States. I hope they will contribute to a better understanding and bring together all men who profess a religious faith, so necessary in the world today and so much more urgent for the confused world of tomorrow."

Dr. Américo Ghioldi, the Argentine educator and member of Congress whom I have already quoted in the first chapter, has this to say on religious liberty:

"When in 1853 the [Argentine] Constitutional Assembly met to draw up the Constitution by which we are governed, one of the fundamental questions to be faced was the following: whether to ratify a fundamental charter with the aim of assuring, maintaining and perpetuating a religious uniformity in the population, even though this might mean a limitation of the number of inhabitants, or whether to fight against poverty, backwardness, and anarchy by adopting the policy of the open door and allowing the free influx of men and things and ideas. Our Constitution was therefore sanctioned on the following line . . . 'to assure the benefits of liberty, for ourselves, for our descendants, and for all men everywhere who desire to live on Argentine soil.'

"Under the protection of this philosophy and these ideals, men of all nationalities and creeds came to our country, in the knowledge that they were protected by a liberal policy founded in religious freedom and sentiments of tolerance and mutual understanding.

"For a good many years, therefore, we Argentines have understood what religious freedom meant to our material and mental progress. The Declaration of May, 1825, clearly stated the principles of our historical evolution. And in the pact of friendship signed during those same years with Great Britain, religious freedom for the English-speaking people was recognized.

"For Argentines, therefore, religious freedom is a living element in our history, and the expression of a fundamental requirement in our final evolution. It has benefited us historically and been a strong factor in our civilization."

John B. Alberdi, the Thomas Jefferson of Argentina, pleaded for a continent without barriers and expressed the views of the majority of the great leaders of the independence movement in South America when he said in his *Bases*:

"If you want to have settlers who are moral and religious, do not foment atheism. If you want families who will help create good private customs, respect the altar that you will find at the center of every belief. Spanish America, limited to Catholicism with the exclusion of other forms of worship, will become a solitary and silent convent of monks. The dilemma is fatal: to become exclusively Catholic, is to remain a thinly peopled country; to be tolerant in religious matters will people our country and make us prosperous. To invite to our shores members of the Anglo-Saxon race and peoples of Germany, Sweden, and Switzerland, while we deny them freedom for the exercise of their own forms of religion, is the equivalent of not inviting them, or it is an invitation in form only or a demonstration of hypocritical liberalism.

"This is literally true. The exclusion of nonconformist faiths from South America signifies the exclusion of Englishmen, Germans, Swiss, North Americans who are not Catholics; that is to say, we shall be excluding the type of settlers that this continent most needs. To bring them to our shores without their religious faith means bringing them without that influence which makes them what they are; it means compelling them to live without religion, to be atheists. . . .

" Is it, by any chance, common sense to desire to foment morality in everyday life and then to proceed to persecute churches that teach the doctrine of Jesus Christ? "

This question, which the great Alberdi asked decades ago, has become pertinent today. Is it wise for the Roman Catholic Church to continue its intransigent attitude toward religious communions that hold in common with it the fundamental tenets of Christianity?

Will the battle for religious liberty have to be fought all over again? Latin America is just one sector of a grave world problem. It is a beach head important enough to shield the mounting of a major offensive the world over by the enemies of real democracy. The issue will have to be faced, not only there, but also in the United States and Canada. If the battle is lost in these two major strongholds of democracy, it will go ill with the cause of freedom in other parts of the world.

An attempt is now being made and directed from the United States to stimulate and mobilize the forces in Latin America that have always been against freedom and democracy. The struggle for religious liberty in Spanish America developed during the wars of independence at the beginning of the eighteenth century. It continues today, even though religious liberty has been written into the constitution of every republic. That supreme liberty is the keystone of the arch of all the democratic aspirations of those southern peoples. Any tampering with it will weaken the whole structure of their national life.

Let it be clearly understood that we are not pleading for religious toleration. We want *religious freedom*. Roman Catholics enjoy freedom, not toleration, in the United States of America where they are a minority. That is the inherited and traditional American conception of what a religious minority is entitled to. Protestants do not want to exist in Latin America, nor anywhere else, by sufferance of the Roman Catholic Church.

We shall next question the right of the Roman Catholic Church to claim South America as its own private fief and shall inquire to what extent our Latin-American neighbors adhere to the faith which that Church represents.

III: How Roman Catholic Is South America?

ROMAN CATHOLICS COMPLAIN THAT PROTESTANTS PROSELYTIZE IN South America. What of it? So does the Roman Catholic Church in this country. It makes a special boast of winning converts from Protestant ranks, and has special agencies for that purpose. Evidently the Roman Catholic attitude can be boiled down to the old slogan: "We may, you mustn't." Protestant missions do not, in fact, exist primarily to proselyte. The picture of missionaries cajoling faithful Catholics to desert their Church is wholly fictitious.

The complaint is based upon the assumption that South America is predominantly Catholic. The Roman Catholic Church arrived in early days with the *Conquistadores,* and it has been there ever since. What need, then, for any other faith? so runs the argument. Do Protestants infer that Roman Catholics are not Christians? If not, then why confuse the people of Latin America by bringing in a rival Christian faith?

This brings us face to face with the question, Is Latin America predominantly Roman Catholic? And the answer is, unhesitatingly, that it is not. The following reasons are given:

1. A very large proportion of the student and educated classes as well as of the new middle class, which is just emerging in Latin America, has not been won to Christianity. These people are traditionally indifferent and even hostile to religion. To be religious or to go to Church is still the sign of inferiority among large numbers of the intellectuals. They threw off the shackles of an obscurantist religious faith weighted with superstition and they have not yet been shown that a man can be a Christian and preserve his intellectual respectability. Will Durant once remarked that "the failure of the Reformation to capture France had left for Frenchmen no half-way house between infallibility and infidelity." Visitors from South America to the United States remark on the ease and naturalness with which religion takes its place in so many aspects of American life. It surprises them to hear prayer offered

at public functions. In his report to one of the leading newspapers of Buenos Aires, a newspaper correspondent from Argentina who recently visited the United States marveled that the president of a great American university should have said grace at a banquet table around which were gathered a group of educators of international repute. The reaction in university centers of Latin America against religion and all that was reminiscent of churchly influence was so radical that all forms of academic garb were barred. It is necessary to go to Protestant countries to find the cap and gown in use.

"In what South American country," asks Dr. Ricardo Rojas in *The Invisible Christ*,[12] " would you find the victorious candidate in a presidential election retiring to his private chamber for prayer on the receipt of the news of his triumph at the polls, as has happened in the United States of America?" This distinguished writer and historian, easily the leading scholar of Argentina, points out the dangerous indifference of the average Argentine to religion. His book is one of the very few written by laymen on the problem of religion that have come out of South America. It is not considered a subject worthy of treatment by an intelligent lay mind. This unique book is a record of a series of dialogues between a visiting bishop and his host, a layman. The prelate has remarked that " the Christian tradition is still living in all the Iberian peoples of the New World." To this Dr. Rojas answers: " The Catholic tradition, as an external form, yes, without doubt; but not the Christian sentiment as an inspiration in life." Later he asserts: " I am not speaking of the indifferent or lukewarm people, but of the bulk of the ' faithful ' and of the emancipated intellectuals when I assert that in the Argentine there never has been any true interest in the religious problem. That is very serious for a growing culture, because a transcendent philosophy gives a setting and an intensity to ideas, not to mention the moral content it might give to political life."

" The intelligent Argentine," says Hubert Herring, in *Good Neighbors*,[13] " expects the women and children to go to mass; his

---

[12] Abingdon Press, 1931. Pages 232, 234, 238.
[13] Yale University Press, 1941.

wife will faithfully aid the pious charities which all good women share, and he will appear upon proper occasion to make the gestures which custom dictates. But the leaders in the business and professional and intellectual life of Argentina no longer accept the claims of the church with any seriousness."

Dr. Juan B. Terán, onetime rector of the Argentine University of Tucumán said:

" How strange it is that we should be able to say that even today there exists in Hispanic American sentimentality something of fetishism, a lack of spirituality, the fondness for external ritual, the devilish beliefs which the superficial Christianization of the period of the Conquest did not extirpate! Men of the upper classes keep aloof from all religious affairs, believing them to be for women only. At best they take up an attitude of benevolent neutrality. They are not atheists, because to be an atheist would be a sign of having reflected on religious problems. They are simply indifferent and Epicurean." [14]

2. Religious illiteracy among the " peon " and rural classes of South America is widespread. Among these neglected peoples Christianity has been rendered almost unrecognizable by the admixture of superstitions and pagan practices.

" Is Chile a Catholic country? " [15] asks Father Alberto Hurtado Cruchaga, Society of Jesus, in a book recently published with full ecclesiastical authority. Father Hurtado is national youth counselor of the Catholic Action in Chile. In answer to the question raised in his remarkably courageous book, he says:

" It is believed that almost every Chilean has some kind of faith. The results shown by investigations and statistics, however, oblige us to think differently. It is true that the majority of our people have a rudimentary religious faith which is expressed by the act of baptism of children, by keeping images in the homes, and by sundry other practices most of which are more superstitious than religious. However, Christian living is every day less apparent and in some regions has even disappeared." [16]

[14] La Salud de la América Española, p. 68, Cabaut, Paris, 1926.
[15] Es Chile un País Católico? Ediciones Splendor, Santiago, Chile, 1942.
[16] Ibid., p. 79.

Father Hurtado quotes a pastoral letter of the Chilean Episcopate of November, 1939, in which the bishops give, as an optimistic estimate, that barely 10 per cent of the population of Chile attends mass on Sundays and feast days.[17] He complains that 50 per cent of the marriages have not been blessed by the Church, and adds: " More than half of the population is therefore born illegitimately in the Christian sense. This percentage is frightening. On the other hand, a basic faith does exist among our people. They possess virtues which are typically Christian and there is a desire to remain close to the Church. Even today, 98.2 per cent have their children baptized which would indicate that the great majority of the population retain a Christian link. Naturally it is understood that the deep significance of baptism is not understood. Some baptize their children to follow a tradition; others to give them a name, or to avoid the evil eye . . . and a very few to make them children of God. As a zealous parish priest, since killed in the earthquake of 1938, once said: ' In Chile there are three sacraments: baptism, confirmation and religious processions.' . . . Our people pay more attention to the worship of the saints and to showy processions . . . than they do to receiving the body of Christ and the forgiveness of their sins." [18]

" Charlie Chaplin is better known in South America today than Jesus Christ," so said a prominent Latin-American writer recently. " Twenty years' use of the cinema has made the comedian better known to the South Americans than four centuries of Roman Catholicism have been able to do for Christ."

The methods which Roman Catholicism employs in dealing with the masses are not calculated to bring men up to the " measure of the stature of the fulness of Christ." That Church upholds a double doctrine of salvation: one for the saint, and one for the common man. Her highest ideal of salvation and preferred methods for achieving it are applied in the monastic orders, which were founded for those who took the Christian Gospel in deadly earnest. For the masses there is a system of inquisitorial supervision, the confessional, the fear of hell and the hope of heaven, a clever scheme of penance and indulgence — a marvelous system for en-

[17] *Ibid.*, p. 80.   [18] *Ibid.*, p. 81.

forcing outward conformity, but no adequate means for lifting
the masses above the plane of childish irresponsibility and invest-
ing them with the dignity and freedom which comes of responsible self-direction.

3. The new industrial classes in Argentina, Chile, and Uruguay have swung away from a Church which they have so
frequently found arrayed on the side of privilege. Only a Church
democratically organized will be able to win these working classes
back to Christianity.

4. Nearly fifteen million Indians in Latin America are waiting
to be Christianized. " Catholicism among the Indians is too largely
a transparent veneer over their primitive practices and attitudes
instead of being a regenerating blood plasma for their souls," said
Dr. Forrest L. Knapp on his return from South America.[19]

This opinion is supported by one of Argentina's most thoughtful writers, Dr. Julio Navarro Monzó, who, at the time of his recent death, held high office in the Ministry of Foreign Affairs of
Argentina and on the editorial staff of the Buenos Aires La Na-
ción. His special interest lay in the problems of religion. Though
liberal in his beliefs he was to the end claimed by the Roman
Catholic Church. In a brochure [20] in which he deals with the concepts of Christ held in Latin America, he has this to say of the
expression of religious faith by the Indians of South America:

" Some years ago in a poor little village of Indians in the mountains of Peru, I stopped to examine a monument similar to many
others which are found by thousands in all Spanish speaking countries. It was a huge stone cross on which was rudely carved the figure of Jesus. At the foot were some flowers and a clay vessel con-
taining an offering of liquor which the Indians had placed there
as an expression of piety. . . .

" Shortly afterward in Lima, I was discussing the subject with
some Peruvian friends, all of them intellectuals, trained in Catholicism, and more or less identified with it, and with a Spanish
artist, an ardent Catholic but intimately acquainted with Peruvian

[19] *The Christian Century*, December 9, 1942.
[20] " Los Conceptos que de Cristo Tiene la América Latina." Reprinted
from *La Reforma,* Imprenta Kidd, Buenos Aires, 1930.

lore. 'When all is said,' I opined, 'lacking a direct knowledge of
the Gospels, which they do not have in their hands, and which
they would not be able to read, since they are illiterate, these
crosses scattered through the mountains of Peru, render a real
service to the natives. They remind them of the tragedy of Calvary; they tell them that nineteen centuries ago Jesus died in love
for mankind; they give them some idea, confused though it may
be of a fact fundamental to the history of humanity.'

"To my surprise, it was the Spanish artist who contradicted me,
with the support of the others. 'You are mistaken,' he said. 'Those
crosses do not remind the Indians of anything like that. The first
missionaries who came to this continent simply destroyed the idols
which the Indians worshipped and told them that in their place
they should worship these crosses. More or less passively the Indians accepted the fact and went on offering to the crucifixes the
same things which formerly they had offered to Pacha-Mama, to
Pacha-Kamac, to Wira Cocha, for the same object and the same
reasons for which they had done it before, — as a prayer to the
unknown and supernatural forces to protect them in danger, to
not be angry with them, to give them prosperity, or, at least, to
leave them in peace. That is all. Of Christianity the Indians know
today exactly as much as their ancestors knew before the Spaniards arrived in this part of the world.'

"My opponent was right, and when one attempts to make a
serious analysis of the conceptions of Christianity which are held
in Latin America, one has to start from that premise. For the immense majority of the inhabitants of those countries which extend from Mexico to Tierra del Fuego, though they are not all Indians, the Christ is exactly what he is to the Indians of Peru, — an
idol, an object of blind and fearful adoration of whom they ask
favors in exchange for offerings. Of the Carpenter, the man of Naz-
areth, they have only a vague idea; of his teachings none at all.

"This I was able to observe at about the same time in which I
had my conversation with the above-mentioned friends, as I
watched in Lima the famous procession of the no less famous image of the 'Lord of Miracles,' a statue of Jesus for which the people of Lima have especial veneration and of which they ask all

kinds of favors, — healing of diseases, success in business, luck in the lottery, happiness in love.

" The same thing occurs in Spain or Portugal, when in Seville they carry through the streets the image of the *Señor Jesus del Gran Poder*, or in Lisbon that of the *Señor de los Pasos*, sorrowfully laden with the cross on the road to Calvary. Thousands of persons, men as well as women, but more women than men, follow these images in procession. With burning tapers in their hands, counting the beads of their rosaries, they form a guard of honor to these painted and clothed images, whose realism rouses a feeling of horror. These statues, however, remind them so little of the central figure of the Gospels, that a young Spanish woman to whom I tried once to explain what Jesus had taught, interrupted me to say, ' What! Then when Jesus was in the world there were already people here? Then wasn't it Jesus who made the world? ' "

5. In 1884 and 1894 laws were enacted in Costa Rica prohibiting the establishment of monastic orders and religious communities. Only recently (in 1943) was that ban lifted. How Roman Catholic is a country that for years has sedulously excluded all religious orders? Repeatedly the Jesuit order has been driven out of several of the Latin-American countries as well as Spain. Argentina has a law prohibiting street religious processions. In that same country priests are disfranchised and cannot vote in public elections. Just how solidly Catholic can countries be which have deprived the Church of all control in the performance of the marriage ceremony and have declared it to be primarily a civil contract? In the majority of Latin-American countries no marriage is legal unless performed by a justice of the peace. After the civil ceremony the contracting parties may seek the blessing of the Church, if they wish. Priests and clergymen who dare to perform a religious marriage ceremony before the civil rite are fined. The claim, therefore, that the southern republics are soundly Catholic will need some considerable qualification.

6. If Latin America is not a legitimate field for Christian missionary activity, why does the Roman Catholic Church itself send missionaries, in ever increasing numbers, to that field?

The indisputable need for missionaries in South America was

pointed out in 1942 by a Belgian Roman Catholic layman and former president of the Belgian Chamber of Deputies, Mr. Frans Van Cauwelaert, who reported with singular candor his impressions of religious conditions in Latin America.[21] He says he was moved by a feeling of wonder at the power and splendor of the work accomplished by the Roman Catholic Church in the early years of its establishment in Latin America. But he was also filled with dismay at the state of neglect in which he found this work and the decline in the religious life itself which that neglect revealed. Among the masses of the people ignorance had developed some remarkable superstitions. Nowhere did he find a sufficient number of priests to meet the spiritual needs of the Latin-American people, and he emphasized the urgent need that other countries should send priests and missionaries to this "neglected continent."

Chile has only one priest to every 3,000 of the population. Peru and Mexico have one priest to every 6,000. Argentina and Brazil have one priest to every 9,000, and Guatemala only one priest for every 25,000 of the population. Compare these figures with the case of the United States of America, where there is one priest to every 3,750 of the total population, and that of England where there is one priest for every 400 Catholics or one for every 7,000 of the total population. These figures reveal the interesting fact that in Protestant countries Roman Catholics are better supplied with priests than in the supposedly Catholic countries of South America.

Comparing Buenos Aires with Philadelphia, two cities of almost equal size, we find that Protestant Philadelphia has 150 Roman Catholic parishes, while the supposedly Catholic city of Buenos Aires has only 84 parishes and 113 churches, and this for a city of 2,300,000.

Latin Americans themselves recognize the spiritual illiteracy of their people. The brilliant editor and writer, Manuel Seoane, whom I have already quoted,[22] when asked how Roman Catholic Latin America was, answered:

[21] "Catholicism in Latin America, Its Passing Weakness and Abiding Strength," in *The Tablet*, London, England, August 29, 1942, p. 102.
[22] For complete statement, see Appendix A.

"I have lived for more than twenty years in Peru, ten in Argentina, six in Chile, and during brief periods in Uruguay, Bolivia, Paraguay, Colombia, Panama, Ecuador, Brazil, and Cuba. I can affirm that, with the honorable exception of a minority which is authentically Catholic, the majority of so-called Latin American Catholics place the trappings and externalities of religion above its deeper and more intimate meaning. . . . Millions of Indians and mestizos in the provinces, where for centuries the Catholic Church has had no competition, have fallen into dead formulism and a meaningless routine. They have missed the living doctrinal content which is the root and substance of true Catholicism.

"I feel that as a Catholic I must say these things. There are millions of Catholic men and women who, like me, are deeply preoccupied over this problem. . . . I was greatly comforted by some of the aspects of North American Roman Catholicism. I was impressed with the modern educational methods of the Sacred Heart nuns of the convent school of Grand Coteau, La.[23] I spent some marvelously peaceful days in that convent, occupying the delightful guest room, the only man in an institution filled with women! This is something that never could have occurred in Latin America."

Dr. Ossorio y Gallardo was sent to Argentina as ambassador by the Spanish republican Government. He resigned when Franco came into power. A distinguished lawyer and man of letters, he was for a number of years president of the Spanish Bar Association, has represented Spain as ambassador in France and Belgium, and at one time was civil governor of the Province of Barcelona. He is the author of several books; his latest, *The World That I Desire*, was published recently in Buenos Aires, where he continues to reside. He is a sincere Roman Catholic. Hence, the significance of the opinions which he here expresses.

"What about Roman Catholicism in Spain and Argentina?" I asked him.

"I will have to express myself somewhat in detail," he said. "But first let me state that there will be nothing theological about

[23] One of Señor Seoane's sisters is a nun in this school.

my replies. I am not a theologian. I have complete respect for the Catholic dogma. I am passionately enamoured of Christ's standard of morals. I do not wish to enter into dogmatic problems for which my preparation is insufficient. I respect the opinions of the Catholic church and I try to confine the expression of my own opinion to those points which I see with absolute clarity and which guide my conscience. This fact should be borne in mind to understand my position and why I attempt to deal with these questions from the social point of view.

" In Spain, the situation of the Catholics is the following: A small minority, mystically inclined, illumined and convinced, profess the Catholic religion with absolute sincerity, purity and blind faith. They deserve the highest respect, because, whether or not they be people of strong intellect, they are without doubt, pure in heart. Another group loves and follows the doctrines of Christ without thought of Catholicism or the Gospel. They guide their lives by the marvelous moral principles that come to them from Calvary. Still another and larger group is composed of those who exploit their religion for their own benefit. They invoke it and pay lip service to it in order to protect their interests, their vanity and their comfort. The immense majority of the Spanish people, particularly the humble classes which are totally indifferent, do not wish to have anything to do with God or His church and do not profess any positive religion. This may seem a harsh statement, but please remember that learned prelates and priests have spoken of the falling away of the masses from religion. That this is true is proved by a recent example. The so-called Catholics are the ones responsible for the war in Spain. They called themselves patriots and welcomed the invasion of their country by foreign troops. They called themselves believers in the law of God and yet coldly executed their brothers during the five years after victory, and many hundreds of them have been imprisoned. They are the self-styled continuers of Spanish history, and yet everything they do is in contradiction to the honoured traditions of Spain. The clergy has lavished attacks against the legitimate regime of the country, with the exception of the Basque priests and those fifty odd priests [imprisoned by Franco] who were photographed in the Carmona

jail surrounding the layman Julian Besteiro, an unbelieving socialist but a good man and virtuous.

"Therefore you will realize that in Spain Catholicism is going
through a great crisis, the outcome of which it is impossible to
predict. If the Catholics were humble, virtuous, poor and just and
contributed with an intelligent effort to social reform, Catholicism
in Spain would reach a glorious culmination. As they are all the
contrary, Spanish Catholicism has fallen to the dust.

"With regard to Catholicism in Argentina, my position as a
guest makes it difficult for me to express myself. But I am afraid
that conditions are similar to those in Spain. The fact that all the
fascists here are Catholics and that they fight liberty and democracy, is a clear indication that they are mainly defenders of
privilege rather than convinced followers of a religious faith. Add
to this the disconcerting opulence of religious ceremonial, the
wealth with which images are adorned, the pomp and magnificence displayed by the Bishops, the luxury with which they surround themselves, the enthusiastic support which the wealthy
give the Church and you will understand the aversion of the working and humbler classes for religion. But please note that I do not
attribute these defects only to Spain and Argentina, but also to
the other countries where Catholics act in the same manner. In
other words, if Catholicism turns entirely to Christ, it will attain
a glorious resurrection, but if it persists in remaining apart from
Christ, it will be condemned to ruin." [24]

It is a trite saying that Uruguay is the most socially advanced
and liberal country in Latin America. There is absolute separation
of Church and State, with not even the concession on the part of
the Government of an occasional gesture of friendship, such as a
Te Deum in the cathedral on special national holidays or the placing of some representative of the hierarchy next to the president of
the republic in group photographs of public events, as so often
occurs even in countries where Church and State have parted
company. In Uruguay the divorce is complete.

Women were granted the vote in national elections seven years
ago (1937). It was thought that this would increase the political

[24] For complete statement, see Appendix G.

influence of the Roman Catholic Church. But the result has been the opposite. The women voters of Uruguay have given their votes to the left wing parties or, at least, to the liberal parties. The *Unión Cívica* is the Roman Catholic party; formerly it had two representatives in the legislature; now it has only one. In the last presidential elections, November, 1942, out of a total of 574,703 votes cast, the Catholic party polled only 24,433. Two women were elected to the legislature, one on the strongly anti-Catholic *Batelista* ticket and the other on the Communist ticket. There is no woman representative of the Catholic party.

Just a few days before my arrival in Montevideo in October of 1943, a committee representing united Protestantism, in Uruguay, presented the president of the Republic, Dr. Juan José de Amézaga, with a Bible. In his speech of acceptance His Excellency said:

" I am deeply grateful to you for the gift of this Bible . . . and I appreciate your visit. You represent a religion that stands for integrity and piety. It is easy to see how much the world is needing these qualities today. They are the foundation stones of civilization and there can be no lasting civilization without this Christian basis. . . .

" I profess no religion, and belong to no church, but I appreciate the importance of religious values. . . . In recalling my student days there is the figure of one man, strong, austere and good, that stands out in special relief. He was one of my professors, and I love his memory because he lived the religious faith he professed. I refer to Dr. Justo Cubiló, one of my teachers in the Law School, who not only taught jurisprudence in those halls of learning, but also the Bible in a Protestant church."

The president next recalled another outstanding representative of Uruguayan Protestantism, who had influenced his life as a young man, Daniel Armand Ugon, pastor of the Waldensian Protestant colonies in Uruguay and founder of one of the first Protestant schools in that country. Dr. Cubiló, to whom the president referred, was for many years a member of the Supreme Court of Uruguay and all through those years taught a Bible class in a Methodist Sunday School.

It is significant that the chief executive of a South American state should be able to declare, without in any way discrediting himself, that he professed no religious faith. One can hardly imagine Great Britain's Prime Minister, or the President of the United States, or the King of Norway, declaring such a fact publicly, even if it were true. Evidently religion in South America does not occupy the vertebral position that it does in the life of these Protestant countries.

There are historical factors that have contributed to the impoverishment of the religious life of the people of Latin America. Let us recall some of these.

In the early years of the colonial period there were devout men in the Roman Catholic Church who were filled with a passion for improving the Indians. There were many devoted priests whose missionary ardor led them through the vast silences of tropical jungles and over the eerie heights of towering mountain ranges. To these saintly messengers of the cross, South America owes a deep debt of gratitude. After all, they brought us the best of our culture; they stood out as shining lights in the midst of very gray surroundings; they planted the seed of true spirituality in the heart of a continent seething with greed and ambition, torn apart by rivalry; they demanded of their converts more than a formal allegiance to the Church; they wanted something more creative than simply an unquestioning obedience to the Church — they were real missionaries, they were in the apostolic succession!

But they were a minority. The Church became a powerful political instrument. Vast amounts of land and wealth came into its hands. Even from early colonial days complaints were heard about the excessive accumulation of material riches in the hands of the clergy. The Inquisition stalked the land — the original " Gestapo," as John Gunther calls it — and every movement of the mind and spirit in the direction of greater freedom or new truth was immediately throttled. These are facts of history and part of the heavy impedimenta with which Latin America commences her career. Hear the verdict of Dr. Javier Prado, onetime rector of the San Marcos University, Lima, Peru, and a distinguished Latin-American Catholic:

" The Spanish priests made callous by the warlike habits which they had acquired along with the soldiers of the conquest; proud of the triumphs gained in the State and among the people by the Christian religion, which now had no foes with which to contend; partly demoralized by the laws that granted them all kinds of privileges; made fanatics by the dominance of religious intolerance; and thirsting for power and rule — this clergy which established the Church of Christ in the Indies, failed to include in its ministry the gospel standard of meekness and humility. . . . Ah, if the Christian Church in America, faithful to the origins of its traditions, had shown in the cities examples such as those which I would be the first to admire; if in the remote country districts it had dedicated itself, as it ought to have done, to the moral redemption of the Indian . . . how great would have been the benefits for which our country would have to thank it! . . . Unfortunately, such things have not been done."

Some extenuating circumstances may be pleaded as a reason for this tragic spiritual failure. First of all, the Vatican was not responsible for the government of the Church in Latin America during the colonial period. When the New World was discovered the papacy gave all of Spanish America as a gift to the crown of Spain, and Brazil went to Portugal. The crown controlled all ecclesiastical affairs. When some high office had to be filled, the monarch presented candidates, and the Vatican had to choose its bishops and archbishops from them. This is the law of *patronato* (patronage) and it holds to this day in most South American countries. The Spanish kings gave wise laws and framed generous statutes, some of the most generous that were ever conceived for the care of the Indians. But the distance from Spain to the colonies was great and the king's representatives not always upright; so the enforcement of these laws was very deficient. If this was the case in matters more closely related to interests of government, how much greater was the failure when religious affairs were involved!

Secondly, the Church had a complete monopoly of the religious situation. In things of the spirit as in things material, the principle of monopoly has had and will continue to have most unhappy results. In isolation the Church went to seed. Christianity during those early centuries in Latin America did not come in contact with the currents of religious awakening that were bringing new life to the Church in France, Great Britain, Germany, and other northern countries of Europe. Even the irritation of a little Protestantism might have helped the overrich and overpowerful Church of the colonial period to become a better Church. Do you remember how A. J. Cronin puts it in *The Keys of the Kingdom?* [25] Francis, as a seminary student in Spain, goes off on his long walk escapade. Father McNabb acknowledges that he is a " queer mixture " in his character. " He's a complete individualist."

" Individualism is rather a dangerous quality in a theologian," Father Tarrant interposed acidly. " It gave us the Reformation."

" And the Reformation gave us a better-behaved Catholic Church," answers Father McNabb.

It is no exaggeration, therefore, to say that Latin America is still a mission field. It is a needy field also as regards health and medical assistance. The first medical laboratory ever organized in the Americas was established in Brazil. But Dr. Charles Morrow Wilson, in *Ambassadors in White*,[26] points out that Spanish America is still harassed by infective diseases, and disease germs cannot be forced to recognize national boundary lines. " Hemisphere solidarity cannot be built on a sick man's society," he says, and then advocates that the United States spend $350,000,000 to help Latin Americans to conquer their health problems.

The spiritual health of Spanish America is also in need of help. We are convinced that hemisphere solidarity cannot be built on a morally sick man's society. Nowhere is Christianity so devoid of inner content or real spiritual life as in Latin America. There is a vast difference between the Latin-American Catholic Church and the Roman Catholicism of northern Europe or North America.

Never has Christianity had such a magnificent missionary opportunity as was given the Roman Catholic Church in the period of the conquest and colonization of the Indies, as Latin America was then called. The field was wide open, support from the civil

[25] Little, Brown, 1941.   [26] Pages 21, 25. Holt, 1942.

authorities was complete, no other rival Church was on the ground, there was no opposition. And yet, after four centuries of undisturbed possession, the Christianization of the continent still lags. It is, therefore, no exaggeration to say that Latin America is Christianity's most shocking failure.

If Roman Catholicism is as important and extensive in Latin America as the hierarchy maintains, then why is it that for all the Latin peoples, from the Rio Grande to the straits of Magellan, there is only one representative in the College of Cardinals? Among the fifty cardinals now in the Roman Catholic hierarchy, thirty are Italians; four, Frenchmen; two, Spaniards; two, Germans; one, Canadian; one, Irish; one, Argentine; et cetera. For the twenty Latin-American countries, the same consideration as for little Ireland: one cardinal (an Argentine), while Protestant Canada and the United States have three between them. Latin America is a field that has been seriously neglected by Roman Catholicism itself. It seems to have been forgotten by the Vatican until the Protestants discovered it. There is no doubt that the Vatican is distressed over the spiritual condition of Spanish America, and efforts are being intensified to correct the religious backwardness of those otherwise brilliant and progressive people. Catholic missionaries are now going from the United States to Latin America. The recent invitation of the National Catholic Charities in the United States to representatives from the southern republics for " in service training " in the United States aims at modernizing the backward Spanish American Church. And nothing but panic could explain the sudden violence with which the hierarchy has struck out at Protestant missions in those southern lands.

American Protestants claim no superiority over their Latin-American friends. They would simply acknowledge the richness of their Christian heritage by sharing it with their neighbors. They recognize the truth of that statement of the great Christian philosopher of Spain, Don Miguel de Unamuno, made to a Uruguayan educator: " Your problem in Latin America is that of fertilizing the spiritual soil. Flowers may grow under the snow, but never in the sand. Life in your America needs to be enriched with spiritual humus."

IV: Catholic Action in Spanish America

" WHEN YOU EAT, GET YOUR FULL SHARE OF VITAMINS AT ' THE SIGN of the Honest Sausage,' " was the advice spread in glaring letters over the front of a new lunchroom on Calle Florida, the fashionable and aristocratic street in the heart of Buenos Aires. A world-famous street, it is lined by the choicest shops, and every day from four to eight it is closed to all vehicular traffic and open to the *boulevardiers*, academicians, pampered sons, professional army officers, and pretty girls who make it one of the world's most picturesque thoroughfares.

The new restaurant with its garish sign almost started a riot. Vitamins, " hot dogs," and Hamburgers on Calle Florida! It was a delightful experience to the crowd who entered to sample the succulent Argentine meats, but an unpardonable affront to the conservatives — that group which with amazing virility tries to beat back the tide of modernism which they see brutally invading their wonderfully gracious but wonderfully selfish world. " Hot dogs " and Hamburgers on Calle Florida, and next door to Mappin and Webbs'! The enticing fragrance of "honest sausage " mingling with the discrete polish of patrician silverware! The vigorous protests of the fastidious customers of the famous store compelled the restaurateur to install a better ventilating system. Later, the police compelled him to take down his too-sensational sign.

The incident is a symbol of the battle that is being waged, not only in Argentina, but in all Latin America. On the one hand a world of change: motion pictures, political liberalism, birth control, women's "rights," popular education, socialism, spiritism, theosophy, Christian Science, and Protestantism; on the other hand the aristocracy, the landowners, the " first families," the religious hierarchy who fear this New World influence and hate the tide of modernism that is spoiling their secluded world and who blame democracy and Yankee influence for it all! Hence the growing intolerance of the Catholic Action in Spanish America.

One of the outstanding leaders of the Argentine Federation of University Students said to the writer: "Peru has a military government backed by the Roman Catholic Church; Castillo's Argentine government, which was deposed by the military revolution of June 4th, was a conservative, landowner's government backed by the Church; today we have a clerical-fascist government supported by the military." A recent issue of the Argentine students' underground paper, *La Voz de Mayo,* makes the following comment:

" The military dictatorship is planning to impose the State religion by Government decree. It is alleged that the blunders and corruption which have characterized government in our country are due to an absence of religion. But we would like to ask a question: Were not the men of the former government, who were deposed by the sword, men of religion? Did they not swear on the Bible to support the Constitution. Nevertheless, they stole, they perjured themselves, they dishonored their investiture. . . . What is the good of religion?"

The most bewildered and uprooted group in Latin America is the student body. They have seen aspects of the traditional religion which make them distrust it; but they do not know where to turn for that which will satisfy their spiritual longings. At the South American conference of university students, held in Santiago, Chile, during August of 1943, the Paraguayan delegation proposed that one of the topics of discussion be: " Clerical Action in America." The Brazilian delegation, officially hand-picked and on a Government junket, opposed the discussion of every subject that had to deal with the Church or with dictatorships. One is shocked at the bitterness against religion which was voiced repeatedly by some of the delegations. The Bolivian delegates declared that the clergy in their country "was not only reactionary but was still living in the days of the cave men." At the final banquet many of the students took offense because Bishop Caro, of Chile, was given a place of honor at the speakers' table.

The student leader I quoted above said: " I belong to a Catholic family, but I cannot help recognizing what an acute problem the invasion of priestly influence in academic circles has created.

The great student reform movement which has spread all over Latin America was launched at the University of Córdoba in 1918 with the battle cry: 'Priests, no; dogmas, no!' The Argentine Nationalist Student Group is a great menace. Their symbol is the Cross and the Sword. They favor isolation for Argentina. Against this reactionary nationalism the third National Congress of Argentine University Students, held in October of 1942, in representation of 45,000 students, supported unanimously a resolution condemning the meddling of the Church in political affairs. In some sections of our country a teacher cannot get a job unless he or she is a member of the Catholic Action."

It is fear of the growing political power of the common people and an unwillingness to keep step with the "march of time" that leads the conservative classes of Spanish America to turn to the army and Church for support in a world that is tumbling about their ears.

Mr. Harold Callender, after an extended tour of South America, reported widespread hostility against the United States on the part of Catholics throughout the continent. "The Catholic suspicion of the United States," he wrote in *The New York Times*,[27] "is so deep and so widespread as to constitute in nearly every one of the South American countries a serious obstacle to Pan-American understanding and, consequently, to collective defense." Roman Catholics in the United States explain this by saying that it is the fear of the anti-Catholic influence of the United States "and the only evidences of any such influence are the American missionaries." Were this true, American priests, who in Latin America are fond of boasting of the power and growth of Roman Catholicism in the United States, could easily allay the fears of their Latin coreligionists. But the cause lies deeper than the disturbing presence of a few hundred American missionaries spread out over a vast continent. It is the fact that the Catholic Church in the southern republics is intensely Hispanic in its sympathies. The vast majority of the members of the monastic orders are Spaniards and Italians. Of the 1,615 priests in Chile,

[27] August 3, 1941.

700 are foreign-born. When a Spanish commission visited Peru in 1942 on the occasion of the Pizarro festivities, it reported on its return to Spain that Peru still held the mother country in great affection, but that the greatest loyalty to Spain was to be found in the convents and monasteries, "in all of which photographs of General Franco were displayed." In the Dominican monastery of Lima, so says the report, "the monks received us with the Falange song." Of course they are strongly anti-Yankee. It is not fear of anti-Catholic influence in the United States, but fear of the United States itself, fear of the American spirit, the spirit of youthfulness and modernity, of freedom and belief in popular education and democracy, which moves the Catholic Action in Latin America.

When General Ramírez, of Argentina, broke off diplomatic relations with the Axis, he was opposed, not only by the reactionary "Colonels' clique" within the army, but by the Church as well. The only civilians in his cabinet were militant Catholics and members of the Catholic Action. One of these, Gustavo Martinez Zuviría, was minister of public education. He is the well-known Argentine author who writes under the pen name of Hugo Wast. Three very bitter anti-Semitic novels have come from his pen. His strong Hispanic leanings make him decidedly anti-American. His appointment was hailed with glee by the Franco press of Spain. One paper emphasizes his " refined Catholic spirit and his love for Spain." *Arriba*, the official Spanish Falange organ, said: " He is a cabinet minister of the first order, a model family man, a faithful patriot, a hammer and tongs Catholic and an ardent lover of Spain." His first decree upon entering office was to make Roman Catholic teaching compulsory in all public schools. The same decree made coeducation illegal for students over thirteen years of age. It was not long before liberal professors were being dismissed from Argentine universities.

Zuviría, the Churchman, resigned from his cabinet position when Argentina broke with the Axis. He represented the Church's repudiation of the Ramírez Government. The withdrawal of this clerical support so weakened that Government that it was easily overturned. In none of the countries of Latin America, some of which are enslaved by cruel tyrannies, has any protest come from the hierarchy against dictatorships which, as Dr. Velasco Ibarra, the new president of Ecuador, has recently said, "corrupt the people. Dictatorships accustom people to be always manipulated by a paternalistic power." The Roman Church has a natural bias to authoritarian forms in State as in Church. There is much to suggest that democracy and Roman Catholicism do not march very comfortably together.

Recently the bishop of Tucumán, Argentina, in view of the antidemocratic activities of so many priests and Catholics, warned that totalitarian principles are contrary to the teachings of the Church. Other Catholic authorities have accused Padres Puig and Wilkinson, who were President Ramírez' closest advisers, of defying Cardinal Copello, of Buenos Aires, by continuing to play politics. The cardinal is said to fear that popular reaction against the present regime may be turned, as in Mexico and Spain, against the Church, so many of whose prelates and priests are back of the present dictatorship. But these isolated voices advising caution have not changed the situation. Priests have been given special broadcasting privileges. They harangue the soldiers in their barracks on the Communist and labor perils. Recently the Virgin Mary was made an honorary general of the army. She receives no salary but is assigned from the public treasury a "viaticum" of ten dollars a day, which, of course, is collected by the Church.

An editorial published in November, 1943, in *El Pueblo,* a leading Church organ in Buenos Aires, makes very clear the principles that are to inspire Catholic Action in Argentina as elsewhere in Latin America. " Our traditional religious unity must be the basis of true national unity," said the editorial. " This compels us openly to combat the enemies of this unity. Protestantism, with its skillful, consistent systematic penetration, is the first enemy of our Roman Catholic ancestral unity. There should be no ill-advised tolerance. We cannot be tolerant toward those whose aim is to break our religious unity and to divide us. . . . Masonry is another of the irreconcilable enemies of our national unity. . . . This is a hidden force allied with all the enemies of Christ."

When I asked Alejandro Carrillo, head of the Labor University in Mexico City which is doing much to educate the working classes, to what extent Mexico was a Catholic country, he answered:

" Most of our people have a Catholicism *sui generis*. An orthodox Roman Catholic from Europe or the United States would hardly recognize his religion in the practices and worship of many of our people. Take away from many of our communities the religious fiestas and the folk dances, and the main support of their religion would be gone. We were all born under the Catholic faith. But very few really practice it. One village with its saints will fight against another which goes out to battle with its particular saint! "

He pointed out that the history of Mexico had been a continual struggle against the Church, but not against the religious sentiment of the people.

While the writer was in Mexico City, an impressive religious procession of Catholic workingmen was organized to visit the virgin of Guadalupe. Religious processions are prohibited, and it was interesting to see the Roman Catholic Church defying the Government by violating the constitution. Recently one of the leaders of the reactionary party declared: " Yes, we are violating the Constitution of the Republic. . . . It (the Constitution) is contrary to the sentiment of the people." I noticed that the five priests who preached during the masses held at the end of this pilgrimage were all Jesuits.

" It is false to say," continued Señor Carrillo, " that the Constitution in a spirit of persecution and partisanship, prohibits the Church to own property. The Church is forbidden to hold property because in Mexico history shows that when the Roman Catholic Church was the leading proprietor of the country her wealth was that of the ' dead hand,' and the economic life of the country was stifled. Religious processions are forbidden because in Mexico they are not processions of believing Catholics but political manifestations of the reactionary party against the Government and national progress.

" The *Sinarquist* movement," said Señor Carrillo, "was pro-Nazi until Pearl Harbor. But on the ninth of December Salvador Abascal, its leader, resigned. There was no assembly or meeting for the election of a successor. Torres Bueno took his place. Behind the scenes the authorities of the Church were making the necessary changes in the *Sinarquismo* which the events of Pearl Harbor made necessary. The hierarchy perceived that the outcome of the war was going to be very different from what they had supposed. There is a private military school not far from Mexico City, and we have discovered that the principal and some of the professors are Jesuits. They are asking the government to recognize the validity of the diplomas they grant. They are training young men to become army officers. The hierarchy is working sedulously to win over members of the army. But the government is aware of all this. You may have noticed a recent decree prohibiting members of the armed forces from wearing their uniforms when they enter a Church."

The essence of the *Hispanidad* movement was never revealed more clearly than in a circular issued in October of 1943 by the director-general of education for the Argentine Province of Tucumán. The communication imparts instructions for the observation of Columbus Day, October 12, in the public schools. Among other astonishing statements is the following:

" America was born under the banner of Spain which gave the new world its religion, its language and its race. Thus did Europe reach America and where these three gifts are not present continental Europe is unknown and the Catholic-Latin spirit is absent. . . . The discoverers of America made it possible for the new continent to enter history and to participate in European culture. From that culture have come the highest spiritual values and a continuation of the Greco-Roman tradition. Thus a way was opened that led America to the Cross and placed her under the aegis of Catholicism. . . . America, therefore, must realize her destiny first of all within Roman Catholicism with which Spain baptized her and civilized her. *Whatever is outside of Catholicism is not American. Protestantism, which is the antithesis of Catholicism, is not American* [italics ours]. . . . America must continue to deepen its culture, and as the only culture that is vitally accessible to us is European culture, we must not sever our connections with it. . . . Apart from Europe, there is no salvation for our culture." Here, as we have said, is the essence of the *Hispanidad* movement. It means everything that would carry Latin America away from the influence of the United States and back to Spain and the Middle Ages.

A few days later the courageous Buenos Aires daily *La Prensa* had a strong editorial referring to this "strange document," as it called the circular. It pointed out that European culture had been enriched by sections of Europe that are not Catholic; that compliance with the instructions of that document would revive the spirit of intolerance and kindle again the fires of religious wars. Did the author not know, asks *La Prensa,* that European culture long ago repudiated such ideas? The editorial then adds: " Among the millions of men who came to our country in the early days and who have enriched it were representatives of all religious faiths. The presence of these men and their descendants, many of whom have remained faithful to the religion of their elders without any weakening of their patriotism, is sufficient to prove the fallacy of the statement that only that which is Catholic is American. Everything that inspires love for freedom, right, and justice is American and will spurn all separatisms based on differences of ideas or creeds. It is regrettable that such aggressively reactionary aberrations should find an echo in Government circles."

It is this Fascist influence on the clergy of Latin America that is very ominous for the future. The Catholic masses and middle class are soundly democratic, but their leadership cares little for real democracy. John T. Whitaker says: [28]

"Since their victory the Franco Spaniards have worked against us in every country of Latin America. . . . Spanish embassies and consulates served as espionage centers. . . . More than a hundred Franco diplomats went into Germany for special schooling in German espionage before they were sent into Latin America. They helped the Germans turn countries like Argentina against us. They spread German propaganda against the United States among the Catholic clergy and the reactionary business elements of the Americas to the south."

In September of 1943, just a few weeks before the writer visited

[28] *We Cannot Escape History,* p. 121. Macmillan, 1943.

Peru, a group of Protestants were holding a Sunday-afternoon service in a large park some distance from the center of the city of Lima. For the last twenty years this group had been carrying on its quiet work in the same spot with full police authorization. But on this particular afternoon they were attacked by a group of young Roman Catholics known as the "Eucharistic Crusade in Defense of the Faith." The Bible was taken by these fanatics and publicly burned in the street.

In no country of Latin America has religious liberty been restricted as in Peru. Not a single liberal paper is published, and the liberal party, known as the *Apra,* has been disfranchised. The strongly centralized military government is stanchly supported by the Roman Catholic hierarchy. In fact it is currently said that Msgr. Cento, the papal legate, is one of the small oligarchy that governs the country. He is an Italian and was Dictator Gomez' strong support in Venezuela. He left that country when Gomez' last illness presaged his death. During the violent public demonstrations of relief over the end of the brutal dictatorship in Venezuela, the crowds that thronged the streets of Caracas called for many heads, among them, so I was told, that of the legate who had, in the meantime, fled to Ecuador.

The clerical tendency toward the repression of freedom of criticism secured from the Government of Peru a most stringent press law, regulating with extreme severity all kinds of written or published propaganda. Article 41 says: "Any act classified as a transgression of the law by our Penal Code, perpetrated by means of addresses, speeches, lectures or threats delivered or pronounced in public places or meetings . . . or by printed matter which is sold, distributed or shown in public places or meetings . . . shall suffer the penalities established in the Penal Code." Article 45 further declares that "any one who offends the Catholic religion or morals . . . by means of the methods enumerated in Article 41, shall be punished by imprisonment from two days to two years and a fine equivalent to his income for a period from two to sixty days."

These and other articles of this severe law are constantly being invoked to secure police help in preventing the sale of Bibles and the holding of Protestant religious services.

In the light of these facts, it is therefore doubly significant that voices should have been raised in the Peruvian congress and that strong editorials and articles should have appeared in the public press condemning the persecution of the Protestants and defending them in the exercise of their constitutional rights.

On October 5, 1943, the following protest signed by five of its members was presented on the floor of the Peruvian senate:

" Mr. President: In the session of August 27 of 1940 of this Senate it was agreed to communicate with the Minister of Government, asking him to reprimand and punish the subordinate police authorities who had exceeded their authority in their relations with the Protestants. He was also asked to protect the latter in the exercise of the rights which our Constitution affords them. Since that date unfortunate incidents have continued to occur with disconcerting frequency. This makes it necessary for us to act again, not in defense of a religious creed, but in behalf of such elementary principles as freedom of expression and of conscience."

The senate statement then quotes from the Catholic magazine, Verdades, of September 18, in which reference is made to the crusade against Protestant work in Peru. The article boasts that this crusade " silenced the heretics in their public park meetings; next a group of enthusiastic young people are dedicating themselves to the task of locating these Protestant groups and then with the support of the police applying the law to silence them."

The senate protest then continued: " While millions of men are sacrificing their lives on fields of battle in defense of liberty and democracy, and when declarations like the Atlantic Charter, to which our Government has expressed its adherence have been made, we cannot believe that the time is favorable for inciting to religious strife. Concerned as we all are in the great task of uniting mankind to face the disastrous consequences which war produces, the present is surely no proper time to deny to foreigners or nationals the most elementary human rights. It is certainly not the wisest time in which to expose ourselves to the severe and justifiable criticism of this attitude which has already been made by the press in some of our neighboring countries.

" Let it not be said in defense of this persecution, that Protestant activity is inimicable to the country's best interests or distasteful to its people. It has been and is, on the contrary, most beneficial. Up in the mountain regions and especially in the Department of Puno, many are the Indians whom the Protestant missionaries have led out of the most abject ignorance, weaning them from the vices of alcohol and the use of the coca leaf. In other sections of the country also their work is worthy of the highest praise. If our government is not able to support and help such valuable work, it, at least, should feel deeply grateful for what it has accomplished, and that gratitude should express itself in granting these missionaries every possible guarantee of freedom of expression, of reunion and of conscience.

"These considerations oblige us to request the Honorable Senate to communicate to the Ministry of Government our desire that immediate and energetic steps be taken to prevent subordinate authorities from continuing to commit these abuses against the Protestants, and that the latter be given full guarantees for the free execution of their religious acts; and furthermore, that the Minister of Foreign Affairs be requested to send out instructions that the passports of persons desirous of coming to Peru, receive the necessary consular visa without any reference to the religious creed which said persons may profess.

"Lima, October 5th, 1943

"(Signed)   Raul A. Pinto

"Pedro Ruiz Bravo

"Francisco Pastor

"Carlos A. Barreda

"Victor F. Baca." [29]

Of the twenty-two members of the Peruvian senate, nineteen voted in support of this resolution. A similar protest against this persecution of the Protestants came from the chamber of deputies.

An encouraging confirmation of our conviction that at heart the Latin-American people are democratic and liberal is the outspoken condemnation by the Peruvian press of this outbreak of fanaticism. One paper in an editorial says:

---

[29] Published in the Congressional records and in the prominent Lima daily *El Comercio*.

"Happily, for more than thirty years, Peru has had religious liberty. It was a victory won at great cost and one which we should not forfeit through carelessness. . . . And although our Constitution declares that the State is to protect the Roman Catholic religion, which the majority of our population professes, it is in duty bound to adopt a neutral attitude in relation to other faiths giving them their full constitutional rights.

"The Catholic Church has rightly protested against the persecution of her priests and prelates in Germany, and the sympathy of the world has been with her in that protest. It cannot now be possible that a small group of Peruvians should imitate and copy such religious persecutions and adopt an attitude which they have condemned in others."

The foremost paper of Callao, Peru, had a leader on the Bible-burning incident which is very strong in its condemnation. It appears under the title: "It is necessary to cross out this crusade." (There is a delightful play on words in the Spanish version: *Hay que cruzar esa cruzada.*)

It refers to the protest lodged in the chamber of deputies and the senate against a movement that would have Peruvians take a "formidable step backwards." "These lion-hearted crusaders," it says, "have found nothing better to do than to attack a Protestant chapel, carry out the Bible and burn it in the street, as if we lived in times of the Holy Inquisition! . . . They are out after the Protestants with the same energy that they would hunt wolves! But what if their guns backfired? . . . What a blot upon our culture are these persecutions! The world will think that we are Kafirs!

"Furthermore, it must be remembered that the evangelicals — whose religious creed we are not now defending nor attacking — are performing a singularly vital service to our country, especially out in the Indian regions, fighting against illiteracy. They have established schools in which they teach the Indians the principles of a civilized life, freeing them from their vices and transforming them into useful members of society.

"This work of the Protestants, far from angering these ' crusaders ' should encourage them to emulate the Protestants. A stupendous crusade which they could organize would be that of getting our priests not only to imitate the Protestants in this social service activity, but to improve on them, and to follow the very meritorious example of our own Catholic missionaries who work in the jungles. . . . Let each priest, in his community, become a teacher, inculcating knowledge that would be beneficial to his flock. That is the best method for displacing the evangelicals. . . . Give, instead of taking away. That is the secret. But assaulting, striking and burning will only produce similar destructive reactions. In a civilized country those methods cannot and will not prosper." [30]

Just before the writer left Lima a call came inviting him to the chamber of deputies. A group of its members had heard that he was investigating the problem of religious liberty. He found a group desperately ashamed of what was happening in their country.

" *Es un anacronismo!* " (It is an anachronism!) exclaimed one of them in disgust.

They wanted the outside world to know that Peru stands for religious freedom. One of the deputies, who represents a district in the Indian country, said:

" We shall never be able to repay the Protestant missionaries for what they have done for our Indians. These missionaries take their wives with them and establish a Christian home in the Indian country. Usually the wife has some training as a nurse. They teach the Indian how to build a better home, how to cultivate his garden, how to improve and balance properly his diet. They teach him not to be ashamed of being an Indian. They awaken in him a sense of human dignity."

This incident is one of many that reveal the strong reaction which is developing among the liberal forces of Spanish America against the monopolistic pretensions of the Roman Catholic hierarchy.

[30] *El Callao,* Callao, Peru, October 13, 1943.

V: Do Latin Americans Resent Protestant Missions?

WHEN THE WRITER REACHED COLOMBIA, HE HAD ALREADY VISITED SIX countries and interviewed hundreds of people in various walks of life. One thing was proving embarrassing: Everyone who had been interviewed, with the exception of three Roman Catholic bishops, was friendly to Protestant work. It was going to appear as if only those persons were interviewed of whose favorable opinion we were assured. It was with a feeling of relief that the interviewer finally found in Bogotá, Colombia, a man in an influential position who did not hesitate to takes sides against Protestant mission work. He was Don Gustavo Uribe, director of Primary Education. Here is a brief summary of the main points of our long conversation in a quiet corner of one of Bogotá's cafés — at three in the afternoon, before the crowds began to troop in for cups of savory Colombian coffee, the best in the world!

"Colombia," he said, "is a Roman Catholic country, and our school system is Roman Catholic. Our women are loyal to the Church. Among the men a certain indifference creeps in as they come in contact with the secular world." He had spent two years in the United States. He had noticed that people went to Church more faithfully and generally there than in Colombia. He also detected a difference between American and Colombian Roman Catholics. The former seemed more fervent, more sincere. "To what is that difference due?" I asked. To better education, he thought. There is a more generally developed culture in the United States. "How would you account," I asked, "for the fact that Roman Catholicism is better and more spiritual in Protestant countries like the United States, England, and parts of Germany?" Again he thought that it was a matter of education; the countries I had mentioned had greater educational facilities. "Could the difference not be due in part," I said, "to the presence and stimulus of a live Protestantism?" He did not know about that. "Do you think Protestantism has a mission to fulfill in Colom-

bia?" I next asked. "No," was his answer. "What good would it
do to change people's religion?" I told him that Protestants would
deny that they were attempting to "change" the religion of the
people. One might "change" from one religion to another and be
neither a better man nor a better Christian. I pointed out Protestantism's interest in developing "personal religion," religion as
an experience rather than as a creed, or a formula, or a ceremony.
He thought that Roman Catholicism would improve itself without
any outside stimulus. Protestantism, he thought, would never ac-
climatize itself among the simple, country people. Catholicism
represented the only type of religious life of which these people
were capable.

I was very grateful to Señor Uribe for his frank statement. He
must have suspected that he was arguing against my position. The
poise and equanimity that characterized this conversation and
the friendliness with which we parted are a token of the kindly
relations that are possible between cultured Protestants and Catholics.

This same spirit of courtesy prevailed in my interviews with
three prominent leaders of Argentine Roman Catholicism: Cardinal Copello, Bishop De Andrea and Bishop Caggiano. The latter
is a distinguished and highly respected prelate, the bishop of Rosario and the head of the Catholic Action in Argentina. When we
parted, there were tears in his eyes: "God bless you," he said; "I
am trying to be a good shepherd to the flock of Jesus Christ." And
I said to him, "My regret, señor obispo, is that I am not able to
call you my bishop!"

Bishop Caggiano's arguments against Protestant missions were
the following: National unity can be secured only on the basis of
religious uniformity; Protestant teaching destroys this religious
uniformity; Protestant proselytism is negative — it deprives people of their inherited faith and is unable to give them a better sub-
stitute; religious freedom is for the foreign colonies that live in
Argentina, but not for propaganda among Catholics: Argentina
resents being considered tierra de misión (a missionary field);
North America was able to permit the unrestricted entrance into
her territory of priests and representatives of other religions

(among them the Roman Catholics) because the groups that professed the different faiths were large, but no such large dissident groups exist in Argentina.

One statement made by him immediately drew my attention. "Why is the United States Government so interested in sending Protestant missionaries to Latin America?" he asked.

I pointed out that the United States Government did not send missionaries. That it was, on the contrary, very difficult to get the State Department to grant a Protestant missionary a passport for travel to Latin America, while all kinds of facilities were given to the Roman Catholic missionaries who wanted to travel to the southern republics. "Furthermore," I said, "there are enough Roman Catholics in Washington to raise a strong protest against any favoritism shown the Protestants by the Government."

In spite of all explanations, he kept insisting that he was puzzled to know " why the American Government wanted to send missionaries to South America." One wonders whether this mistaken idea is based on ignorance of the facts or whether it is a suggestion which is being circulated intentionally over Latin America and with bad faith, by certain propagandists against "American imperialism." One can hardly understand how a distinguished Roman Catholic authority like Msgr. Caggiano should be so grossly misinformed on this point.

The cardinal primate, Archbishop Copello, and Msgr. De Andrea, bishop of Temnos, were very considerate and patient in listening to our questions. Our interviews with them brought us no further light on the Roman Catholic attitude toward Protestant missions but were valuable for the purpose of confirming our understanding of that attitude. Archbishop Copello said: "I have been receiving reports regarding the alarming activity of Protestant missionaries who, with seemingly inexhaustible financial resources, are engaged in an intense campaign of proselytism. At the same time everything is done to discredit the Catholic Church. I do not have exact figures as to the number of these missionaries, but I do know that their activities have seriously molested our Catholic people and, consequently, have preoccupied the authorities of the Church."

When asked if he did not think that the effort to secure Government action to prevent the free movement of Protestant missionaries was a violation of the principle of religious freedom, the cardinal answered:

"I do not so consider it. The Church must watch over the souls committed to her; she must protect them from dangers and evils that may threaten them. Freedom of religion which our Constitution guarantees, is not affected by this attitude of the Church authorities. Everybody in our country is free to practice the religion he prefers, but without attacking the Catholic religion, which the Argentine nation supports according to a Constitutional provision. It is morally obligated also to defend it since it is the religion of the majority."

When he was reminded that the Argentine constitution says only that the "State shall support the Roman Catholic Church," he still insisted that by implication that meant moral as well as financial support and that the Government was obligated to defend the Church against any attack.

On December 18, 1943, the archbishops and bishops of Peru issued a pastoral letter directed against the Protestants, which was ordered to be read from the pulpit in every Roman Catholic Church of Peru. A few extracts from its nearly eight pages (all italics ours) will reveal what the hierarchy in that country thinks of Protestantism:

"We are in duty bound to raise today a warning voice against a grave and widespread danger which seriously threatens the purity and unity of our religious faith. . . . We warn you therefore once more against the multitude of mercenary pastors who have invaded our native land. . . . You will understand ere this that we refer to Protestant propaganda.

"Many years ago now Protestantism commenced to filter through into this nation. The Methodists arrived in 1877; the Independent Sects in 1893; and the Salvation Army in 1910, followed by new groups which now number some two dozen. The first groups, however, worked very much behind the scenes, since the Fourth Article of our Constitution declared the Apostolic Roman Catholic faith to be the state religion *to the exclusion of all other forms of worship.* The Protestant sects, however, in combination with anti-Catholic societies, refused to rest till they had succeeded by *specious pretexts* in inducing our legislative chambers first to mutilate and later to repeal this Article, which constituted *a sacred bulwark of our religious belief and a powerful restraint against sectarian audacity.*

" Scarcely was this protecting wall broken down and liberty of worship granted than the unrestrained violence of the sects overflowed in campaigns to propagate their doctrines; and, as though they now owned the country, they abused the hospitality so liberally extended to them and thought themselves quite within their rights in setting to work to demolish the secular edifice of our Catholicism by applying to it *the incendiary torch of their heretical blasphemy* in order to convert the land of Santa Rosa into a fief of reformed Protestantism. . . . With irritating cynicism we see them posing as teachers of religion, belching forth upon the ignorant populace from their soap-boxes in streets, plazas and parks, the whole content of their falsehood. . . .

" We have sketched some remedies whereby, according to the advice of the Prince of Apostles, we may know how to resist the common enemy, holding ourselves firm in the faith; all united in one purpose of defending our Christian values with a high sense of Catholicity, *denying all co-operation to Protestant work,* in money, support, attendance at its services and schools, reading its literature, membership in its societies, even athletic ones such as the Y.M.C.A. and Y.W.C.A. Beware of false prophets who come to you in sheep's clothing but inwardly they are ravening wolves."

All this is signed by the archbishop of Lima, primate of Peru, and three other archbishops, six bishops, and two apostolic vicars. The latter are direct representatives of the Pope, and their signature would lead to the assumption that this document is in full accord with the policy of the Vatican.

Those who might be inclined to shrug their shoulders and exclaim, " Oh well, that happened in Peru," are reminded by *The Christian Century,*[31] in its comment on this pastoral letter: " Anti-Semitism, whether at home or abroad, is a loathsome social dis-

[31] April 5, 1944. " Ominous Peru."

ease. . . . No thoughtful person is disposed to take an isolationist view of this matter or to assume that anti-Semitism in Germany is something that people in the United States can lightly ignore." And the editorial goes on to claim that, in like manner, intolerant attitudes in the relations between Protestants and Catholics assumed by either group, though it be in some distant land, cannot be a matter of indifference to the people of America.

Not all testimonies regarding Protestant work from Catholic priests in Latin America are derogatory. Referring again to that remarkable book *Is Chile a Catholic Country?* [32] published recently by Father Hurtado, we find in it an interesting estimate of Protestant activities in Chile.

" The most outstanding thing about this Protestant campaign," says Father Hurtado, " is the fervor which animates some of their [the Protestant] preachers and their adherents. . . . It is not a fact that the Protestant movement is first and foremost a campaign made possible by foreign money. The largest part of the money spent in Chile is that of Chileans. The Pentecostals or ' Canutos,' which is a national sect, do not have a single foreign preacher and their expenses are met entirely from the tithes and offerings of their followers.[33]

" A mechanic who joined the Baptists in Talca, converted his second wife and he pays from his own pocket the 100 pesos monthly needed to hire a small room in Valparaíso needed to preach the Gospel. When a hall in Recreo was opened, this modest worker furnished it himself and patiently invited one by one the persons he wished to attract there. At first he was forced to wait for several hours with his small hall empty, while the people went instead to the theatre, but because of his perseverance he has finally been able to get a group together. All of his free time is used ' to save souls,' as he says. What an example for many Catholics who object to giving their time and even their money to really save souls! " [34]

Father Hurtado finally concludes:

[32] Ediciones Splendor, Santiago, Chile, 1942.
[33] *Ibid*, p. 108.
[34] *Ibid.*, p. 120.

"Many people praise the transformation which takes place when souls come into contact with Protestantism: habitual drinkers give up drinking, others become men of prayer. It is a fact, that in many cases they obtain results by perseverance and work, by an untiring and contagious zeal, by contact with the word of God, and because they are able to awaken in men the feeling of responsibility." [35]

"More than a campaign against Protestants, what we need is a campaign for positive Christianity. Let us go to the people and teach them our holy religion, helping them to live it and love it." [36]

Three Chilean ex-presidents have expressed their estimate of Protestant influence in their country. All that I had dared to expect was some general statement that would represent the collective feeling of the leaders of political thought in Chile. But they considered the matter important enough to give it personal attention and, on their own initiative, issued individual and separate expressions of their views. From Ex-President Alessandri's long letter of November 10, 1943, I quote:

"I have no hesitation at all in declaring that as a result of continuous and attentive observation of the work Protestantism realizes in my country, I give it my unstinted applause and recognize that it has always contributed to the progress of our country and the moral improvement of our people. Its schools, its philanthropic and social service activities, its propaganda and its teachings have always been inspired by the highest Christian principles and by the ethical doctrines of love and peace to all men."

Ex-President Juan Esteban Montero, under date of November 17, 1943, wrote in part as follows:

"You ask me to express my opinion regarding the campaign carried on in the United States against the presence of Protestant missionaries in our country. I understand that it is claimed that they are an obstacle to the Good Neighbor policy. I am not acquainted with the arguments on which such an opinion is based; but I think that it is extremely strange that any one should hold

[35] *Ibid.*
[36] *Ibid.*, p. 127.

such an idea in his mind. The very character of the work accomplished by these missionaries would refute any such idea.

" Cordial relations between two countries and a policy of good
neighborliness cannot suffer any harm but, on the contrary, will be
strengthened by any effort which is made to elevate the moral level
of mankind. . . . Protestant missions, with their schools, their
hospitals, their centres of social service, and their preaching, constitute an important contribution to the strengthening of moral
principles in our country. And as they have always avoided meddling in politics, they are a most valuable aid to international
good will and a strong support for the Good Neighbor policy."

Ex-President Carlos Íbañez says, in his letter of October 25,
1943:

" I have been told of the attacks against the Protestant Church
in the United States because of its missionary activity in Latin
America. In these attacks it is alleged that these missions are an
obstacle to the Good Neighbor policy.

" It is my agreeable duty to say to you that, as far as Chile is
concerned, there is no basis or foundation for such an unjust accusation. Protestant methods of work have in them nothing which
constitute an offence to our national sentiment or the culture of
our people. On the contrary, the work which is accomplished by
the Protestant churches is the expression of a practical and disinterested religion which only a very bigoted mind could fail to
recognize.

" The value of Protestant work can be seen in its campaign
against alcoholism, its social work on behalf of the disinterested,
its clinics, orphanages, homes for the homeless, and the high type
of physical development encouraged by the Y.M.C.A.

" And finally, my profound interest in the problem of education
leads me to pay the warmest tribute to such schools as Santiago
College, the Institute Inglés, and the Protestant schools in Temuco.
All these institutions are making a valuable contribution to our
culture.

" May my testimony serve to encourage your missions to work
with more strength and vigor on behalf of our people."

Chile is one of the five Latin-American countries that have governments chosen in free and popular elections. Hence, a statement signed by every member of the Chilean president's cabinet is full of significance.

" The undersigned, being consulted regarding their estimate of the Protestant missionaries who have come from the United States and who work in Chile, on the basis of their observation as ministers of state, declare:

" That the total contribution of these missionaries to our country has been highly beneficial in a cultural, civic, and spiritual sense.

" That the missionaries who have identified themselves with the life of Chile have been faithful interpreters of that sincere friendship which is always a sacred bond between sister nations.

" That, far from creating difficulties in international relations or being an obstacle to the Good Neighbor policy, they have promoted a feeling of mutual understanding and a spirit of practical co-operation without in any way interfering in political matters."

Then follow the signatures of the cabinet members: Juan Antonio Iribarren, Marcial Mora Miranda (Foreign Relations), Dr. Leonardo Guzman (Public Health), Dr. Salvador Allende (Public Health), Arturo Olavarría, Domingo Durán (various portfolios), Guillermo Labarca Hubertson (Education), Luis Alamos Barros (Interior).

Dr. Antonio Sagarna, member of the Supreme Court of Argentina, is one of that country's truly great men. Among the many prominent positions formerly occupied by Dr. Sagarna was that of minister of public education and ambassador of Argentina to Peru. Here is his thoughtful and weighty opinion on the problem under examination:

" The presence of Protestant missionaries is not and cannot possibly be an offense to the people of Argentina in whose history, institutions and daily life freedom of conscience and of religious practice has always been held as something very precious. Eminent Catholics have made their contribution to this tradition.

" Protestantism or the Reformation has made an indisputable moral contribution to the spiritual life of our America. We would be poorer today if to our shores had not come representatives of

British, Swiss, French, Dutch and North American Protestant churches. In this as in all other relations competition revives and purifies.

"Some years ago when I was the Envoy Extraordinary and Minister Plenipotentiary to Peru, I followed the advice of some Peruvian friends, who were not Protestant, and placed my two sons in the Protestant Anglo-Peruvian school of Lima which was under the principalship of an outstanding Christian gentleman, a wise and loving authority on things Spanish and Peruvian and former professor of the San Marcos University, Dr. John A. Mackay, whom since that day I have been privileged to count among my dearest friends. In that school, housed in a very modest building with no chapel or church adjacent, my sons fell under Christian influences which molded their character and shaped their personality without awakening in them any spirit of sectarianism or intolerance. Dr. Mackay enjoyed the highest esteem of conspicuous Peruvian Catholics such as Javier Prado y Ugarteche, Victor Andrés Belaunde, José Matías Mansanilla, Carlos Ledgard, Luis Fernan Cisneros, Cristóbal Lozada y Puga and many others. My daughter attended a Catholic school in Chorrillos.

"Great Britain has sent many and excellent persons and institutions to the Argentine Republic but her best gift during the last fifty years was the apostolic personality of William C. Morris, the most Argentine, the most sacrificial and the most spiritually fruitful foreigner that I have ever known." [37]

Dr. Sagarna recalled how, "in spite of the fanatical opposition of certain religionists, Morris, 'that English Protestant curate,' as they despisingly called him, carried on his great work patiently crowning it ever with a halo of tolerance, justice and love," and how "he never asked any child who came to his schools or any teacher he employed, what their church affiliations were, but rather what their attitude was toward life and what their convictions were regarding life.

"I knew this great man," he continued, "and loved and admired

[37] See Introduction page xx. Morris began his social service work with the Methodists in Buenos Aires, but later, as an ordained clergyman, he worked under the auspices of the Anglican Church.

him as did also Catholics like Tancredo, Enrique and Humberto Pietranera, Lucio Correa Morales, Federico Pinedo (Senior), Angel Gallardo, etc. When as a very poor young man I was starting out in life, I offered to help Morris in his educational work by giving free classes in Argentine history and civics. This was my first job as a teacher and I held it for three years. I am proud to recall this beginning of a friendship which lasted for more than forty years.

"The United States has been to us a model in the matter of child-welfare. No country has expressed its sense of responsibility for the care of its children so eloquently in wise legislation as the United States. No people have been so deeply Christian in their attention to the moral and physical health and needs of their children than the people who inhabit the land of Washington, Lincoln and Horace Mann. It is from that people that we have received our example and our stimulus and they have shown us the way."

Journalists are a highly honored literary guild and an important element in the intellectual life of Latin America. To be a *periodista* gives a man a high standing in the community. Most South American journalists take their work very seriously and the result is that those southern republics can boast of some of the really great newspapers of our day. Conspicuous among them is *La Prensa*, of Buenos Aires. I was privileged to interview a prominent member of its editorial staff whose name shall be omitted. He said it was preposterous to think that Protestant missionaries were an obstacle to the Good Neighbor policy. "I am a Catholic," he added, "and I am deeply disturbed by the fact that the Nazi and Fascist propagandists in this country (Argentina) are Roman Catholics. They are bad Catholics. It isn't against Catholicism that I protest, but against those who use the Church for the support of their totalitarian ideas. Just now, as the influence of the clergy is strong in the government, many who formerly were enemies of the Church are suddenly becoming more bigoted than any bishop.

"There is a noticeable religious difference," he went on to say, "between the United States and South America. I have been in the United States on three different occasions. In spite of its division into the many denominations and sects, there is an ethical content to religion in that country which is all too often absent in this southern continent. For many people here religion is a form, a liturgy, a social convention." He repeated several times: " *El catolicismo es una religión de promesas.*" [Catholicism is a religion of promises.] I did not at first catch the meaning of this phrase. Then it dawned on me that what he meant was that religion for many people in South America was a promise for life after death; it held no promise or had little reference to life here and now. He concluded, " The religion of too many people here has no connection with honesty at the polls or integrity of character in business transactions."

Among the numerous newspapermen whom I interviewed, Dr. Julio Zeballos stands out in special relief. He is managing editor of *La Capital,* of Rosario, the large inland city of Argentina. This paper is the oldest newspaper in that country, and Dr. Zeballos is president of the Rosario " Press Circle." He was astonished to know that anyone should think Argentina would resent the presence of missionaries of non-Catholic faiths. Education, he pointed out, had weaned great masses of people away from religion. " The elemental necessity in every country," he said, " is to grant free opportunity for the expression of all honest political, social, and religious ideas. As a result of this free movement, the best will finally prevail."

Dr. Casal Castel, the distinguished Roman Catholic writer of Argentina, to whom reference has already been made, was asked if he considered that the presence in South America of Protestant missionaries was an obstacle to the Good Neighbor policy, and in answer he said most emphatically: " It is not. I maintain that the work of these missionaries is a form — the most effective form — of that same policy. I would even venture to say that it is a form of solidarity in the spiritual realm. It is a practical Pan-Americanism! For within the family of America there should be no suspicions or misgivings, no offensive distinctions nor exclusions. The day in which America blots out the last frontiers — physical and economic — and suppresses all ' spiritual tariff walls ' we shall have realized the dream of a new world, and we shall have fulfilled the hopes that the old world built on those dreams."

Dr. Hélio Lobo is a member of the Brazilian Academy of Letters and of the Historical and Geographical Institute of Brazil. He was consul general of Brazil in London and in New York, and served as general secretary of the Brazilian delegation to the peace conference of Versailles. He was minister plenipotentiary to Uruguay and Holland and was connected with the International Labor office at Geneva as well as the office of the League of Nations.

"Are American missionaries an obstacle to the Good Neighbor policy?" he was asked.

"Not at all," was his answer. "Those missionaries can only help that policy, as they are, in fact, doing. They preach the Gospel, whose predominant note is that of the brotherhood of all men. It is absurd to think that they do not collaborate in a policy which has as its objective a fraternal relation between the peoples of America."

"What is your opinion of Protestantism in Brazil?" was my next question.

"Protestant missionary work in Brazil deserves our warmest encouragement and praise because of what it has done in favor of education, health and social welfare, especially of the humbler classes of our people. . . . Whoever travels into the interior of our country cannot help but admire the dedication, the self-abnegation and the humanitarian aims of the Protestant missionaries. They have founded schools, raised hospitals, and given helpful instruction, — and accomplished all this in the face of great obstacles and without any applause. It is to be regretted that this good work is not better known."

Dr. Manuel Carlos Ferraz, president of the court of appeals of the State of São Paulo, gathers up in his choice personality the dignity of a grandee and the gentleness and courtesy of a highly refined spirit.

To our question regarding the strength of Roman Catholicism in Brazil, he said: "I shall answer in the words of a Chaplain of King Albert of Belgium who visited our country in 1922. He said: 'An appreciable percentage of the population is faithful to the

Church and practices Catholicism. There is, on the other hand, a large number of indifferent and superstitious people. There is an insufficient number of priests to attend adequately to the indoctrination and guidance of the people. The priests that are available are too reduced in numbers to be able to attend to the religious needs of a country of such vast dimensions as Brazil.' "

To my second question regarding the attitude of Brazilians toward foreign Protestant missionaries, he said:

" Missionaries are in no way an obstacle to the Good Neighbor policy. They are making a most valuable contribution to the moral and cultural development of our country. They help us understand the United States better and they interpret certain aspects of the life of that country to us."

" Should the doors of Brazil be closed to the admittance of missionaries of other faiths? " I asked.

" Protestantism has served as a stimulus to Roman Catholicism. It is a warning to that Church that it must awaken from the sleep of indifference into which it had been lulled as a result of its isolation from other currents of Christian thought. When Roman Catholicism was our State religion and other religions were prohibited in Brazil, Catholicism entered a period of decay. The freedom which was later granted to other religions and the separation of Church and State, have been helpful to the Roman Church itself. She has been compelled to open more schools, create more parishes and dioceses and build more churches."

When I asked him what he thought of Protestantism in Brazil, he answered:

" Protestantism has given Brazil upright and honest men who have been of great service to our country. It has awakened in its followers a sense of responsibility and developed in them a staunchness of character that has become a veritable national asset. It has stirred up in its people a hunger to know and given them a taste for reading. One of Brazil's greatest grammarians was a Protestant." [38]

A significant statement comes to me from an interview with a

[38] For complete statement, see Appendix J.

Brazilian Roman Catholic bishop. It will reinforce the conviction that there is a considerable body of opinion in Latin America that believes that American missionary effort is not an obstacle to the Good Neighbor policy.

Don Carlos Duarte Costa is bishop of Maura and is resident in Rio de Janeiro. He is owner and director of a religious magazine, *Mensageiro de N.S. Menina*. When the dean of Canterbury's book *Soviet Power* was translated and published in Brazil, to the amazement of the public and the horror of the reactionaries, it appeared with a preface by Bishop Duarte Costa. A book praising Russia with an introduction by a Roman Catholic bishop in praise of the book! And, furthermore, the dean of Canterbury is a Protestant!

Bishop Duarte Costa was interviewed and was pleased to make the following statement:

" I do not consider that the coming of Protestant missionaries prejudices the work of Pan-Americanism and the Good Neighbor policy. Our Catholic clergy is not nationalized and any discrimination in the treatment of Churches is odious in countries where the State is secular and separated from the Church.

" In order to secure national unity it was never indispensable to have religious unity. The clergy which comes here does not come with the purpose of carrying on a work of espionage or of realizing efforts contrary to the interests of Brazil. I have never known of any American missionary who was arrested as a spy. What I do know from trustworthy reports, is that their educational work is highly esteemed in our country. These are the reasons why I am of the opinion that there is no harm in the coming of missionaries to our country."

These and many other testimonies that could be presented, if space permitted, serve to indicate that, if any resentment against Protestant missionary activity in Latin America exists, it will be found almost exclusively among the small groups of clerical reactionaries both in South America and in the United States. Others, of course, who will be opposed to missionary work in Latin America are the sophisticated people who have no use for religion. Benjamin Subercaseaux, of Chile, reports a conversation with one of these.

"An atheist friend of mine," he says, "with whom I was discussing this matter, flippantly remarked that we would do well to prevent Protestant missions from spreading other doctrines on the virgin continent of Latin America. 'You poor South Americans are already too burdened with one religion to have to bear another,' he remarked. To a person with an antireligious bias the problem will seem to deserve no more serious attention than that given it by my unbelieving friend. But religion is an ineradicable element in man's life. The Americas have entered a period of good relations and this problem of the relations between different Churches which has arisen to complicate the Good Neighbor policy is more than a simple theological quarrel."

Evidence is abundant that the people of Spanish America welcome the representatives of Protestantism and give them their friendship and support. They value the services of Protestant schools and hospitals. They place their children under the care of Protestant educational institutions. Many of them recognize that the presence of Protestant work is furnishing a salutary stimulus and challenge to Catholic thought and practice. Not infrequently they testify to their regard for Protestant missions by conferring honors upon missionary leaders. In Havana, at a large gathering of civic, educational, and Church leaders, in 1943, Dr. H. B. Bardwell and Dr. S. A. Neblett were presented with parchments by the mayor of the city and made " adopted sons " of Cuba, in appreciation of their long services. Dr. Bardwell has been in Cuba for forty years and Dr. Neblett for forty-one years. In the center of Rio de Janeiro is a wide street which the city council has named Avenue of Erasmo Braga, in honor of a Protestant minister. Dr. Braga was an influential preacher, an educational expert, and a distinguished man of letters. Dr. H. C. Tucker, " an American with the heart of a Brazilian," as he is affectionately called by the people of Brazil, was granted, in 1943, the highest decoration by the Government of Brazil, *o comenda da ordem do Cruzeiro do Sul*. For fifty-six years he had lived in his adopted country, serving as agent of the American Bible Society. Dr. Benjamin H. Hunnicutt, president of

Mackenzie College in São Paulo, was recently honored in the same way.

Protestantism has a host of great and good friends in Latin America. Our next question, therefore, will be: Why is this so? What do our southern neighbors see in Protestantism? And we shall let the Latin Americans themselves answer.

VI: Latin Americans Speak Out

THE STUDENTS OF THE UNIVERSITY OF SÃO PAULO WERE ON STRIKE. Police representatives of the Government had broken up one of their meetings, and they were refusing to return to their classes until the officer responsible for the attack was dismissed. It was interesting to see this student protest and action carried out in the face of a dictatorship. The political tension did not prevent the scholarly and progressive rector of the university from receiving us. Dr. Jorge Americano is a Roman Catholic, a distinguished lawyer, and the possessor of a library that would be the envy of any book lover. He mentioned several facts which are very important for an analysis of our problem.

"Missionaries do not cause any trouble," he said. "There is a minority of the population of our country that is actively and conscientiously Catholic. The great mass of the people are ignorant of the spiritual essence of Christianity. *Friction between the United States and the peoples of South America is due largely to a feeling of superiority on the part of North Americans* [italics ours]. It has nothing to do with being a Protestant or not being one. Wherever American troops, sailors or functionaries are quartered, there you have all the elements necessary for trouble. The Americans are better paid than the rest of the people, they spend lavishly, pay higher prices for everything and so raise the cost of living; they give bigger tips and get better service. Is it any wonder that Brazilians sometimes are resentful? "

Perennial tensions exist between North and South America. Nothing is to be gained by denying their existence. Latin and Anglo-Saxon Americans have not yet succeeded in adjusting their relations harmoniously. And, of course, everyone seeks the reason. The representatives of the Vatican in the United States and Latin America were deeply concerned over the religious indifference of the peoples of the southern republics, and, with their usual astuteness, they were quick to see the advantage inter-American friction gave them in their war upon Protestant missions. They spread the suggestion that resentment was caused by the presence of Protestant missionaries. They assured American businessmen that trade between the two continents would improve as soon as the missionaries were withdrawn. They dropped the hint in American diplomatic circles that the Good Neighbor policy would never prosper so long as Protestant missionary activity continued. And in too many cases the bait was swallowed — hook, line, and sinker. But at last we are beginning to hear from the Latin Americans themselves as they try to tell us very bluntly, in spite of their traditional courtesy, what is the real cause of the friction.

Dr. Americano, whom we have just quoted, says that tensions are produced between North and South Americans by an attitude and feeling of superiority on the part of the former. They spend lavishly, he says; they demand special attention, and they can pay for it. Americans are, of course, irrepressible. Europeans are trained to be more subdued. Britons are usually on guard to do the proper thing. Americans are too frequently unconcerned about the proprieties. Latin Americans cannot quite understand the boisterousness of Americans, especially in public places. No force on earth can contain the ebulliency of the youthful American spirit. Americans *will* boast! And, of course, they have something to boast about. Do they not come from " God's own country "?

As this is being written, Dr. Hernane Tavares, a Brazilian educator who was special adviser to the Co-ordinator of Inter-American Affairs in Washington, is being given considerable publicity because of certain statements he made at the International Education Assembly held at Frederick, Md., in June, 1944. He asserted that relations between the United States and Latin-American countries were deteriorating. He attributed this condition to three main reasons: political, economic, and personal conduct. Notice that he does not mention Protestant missions as a disturbing element in inter-American relations.

Dr. Tavares explains what he means by " personal conduct." The American Government, he is reported to have said, was " pouring officials by the thousands into Latin-American countries with the most disastrous effect," and " the conduct of these officials is all too frquently unorthodox and rowdy." He said that they " spent too much money " and that their conduct alienated them from the Brazilian people.

There are many thoughtful Americans who have lived in South America who recognize that after due allowance is made for any exaggeration in the statements of these distinguished Latin Americans there is too much truth in their complaints. A former United States Minister to Uruguay, Mr. U. Grant Smith, in a letter to *The New York Times,* January 11, 1937, supports the main thesis of these complaints. We quote:

" There remain two outstanding causes of friction for which we are directly responsible. They are, in short, the tactless manner in which some of our government departments have, sometimes regardless of the advice of the Department of State — not that its record is above criticism — all too often taken action which had a direct effect upon the countries to the south of us and, secondly, the unbusinesslike neglect to cultivate outside contacts of members of the so-called American colonies in those countries, which can be said to be the focal point of infection in our relations with Latin American peoples. . . . It is incredible that the executives at the head offices in this country should not long ago have awakened to the fact that many of their employes, though technically efficient, were acting as irritants rather than attempting to cultivate friendship as a business asset. Their airs of superiority would be ludicrous if the results were less serious. We wish most earnestly to increase our commerce with those countries. We want them to act with us politically as well. Yet we seem to get no further than official expressions of mutual esteem, while Americans and their wives refuse to learn the language and to mingle with the society of the places to which their employers have sent them."

Again you will notice that missionaries are not mentioned as sabotaging the Good Neighbor policy. Protestant missionaries do learn the languages and they do mingle in a friendly way with the peoples among whom they live. They establish homes in these lands and spend their lifetime in their adopted country which they have learned to love. One who represents admirably the way missionaries tend to identify themselves with the life of the country in which they labor is Dr. James H. McLean, dean of the foreign missionaries in Chile. He was sent out by the Presbyterian Board in 1906 and he has engaged continuously in the evangelical enterprise until today. Since 1912 he has been on the teaching staff of the University of Chile and a regular radio preacher for the last two years. He has been principal of the large Protestant boys' school, Instituto Inglés, and for a number of years was pastor of the Union Church of Santiago. In a recent letter he expresses his affection for the Chilean people.

" I long for some way," he says, " of expressing my sincere tribute to the host of Chileans who have been hospitable and kindly beyond my fondest hopes. The educated classes, in particular, have admitted me to their confidence and enriching friendship. Without embarrassment we have been able to collaborate in moral crusades and in public service. The Roman Catholic clergy I have known treat me as a brother and fellow-Christian though they do not recede from any of their well-defined positions on ecclesiastical matters. All my students have listened with reverence to my expositions of the Gospel. Many devout Roman Catholics have assured me that they listen to my radio addresses every Sunday morning. My relationships with the Government and authorities have been uniformly cordial and pleasant. The Rotary Club has classified me as a religious worker and has repeatedly honored me with office.

" In all good conscience, especially when I recall the hundred or more students for whom I have secured scholarships in the United States, I can modestly claim to have done something toward fostering fraternal relations between Chile and the United States without having lowered my banner as a missionary."

An American who gives a lifetime of service to another country and who falls in love with it while doing so! Is this a " hurdle " in the way of Good Neighbor relations? Let us ask representative Latin Americans what they think of the work of Protestant missionaries.

José A. Alfonso, or " Don José," as he is affectionately called, has just retired from his official duties as secretary of the surrogate court and professor at the law school of Chile. He is Chile's most prominent and best-beloved publicist and president of the board of primary education. His articles on education and public welfare have always been accorded wide publicity. Perhaps it would be no exaggeration to acclaim him "Chile's Grand Old Man"! Here are a few sentences from his long letter to Dr. McLean:

" My attitude toward the work of North American missionaries is that of absolute support and unstinted admiration. My reason for doing so is that I recognize that they are exerting a profoundly moral influence among our people as well as a deeply Christian influence. . . . This has always been my attitude, and, as a publicist, I have expressed it on every opportunity that I had.

"You will remember that when you were principal of the Instituto Inglés [39] I placed my son in that institution not only because I wanted him to have the benefit of an English education, but also because I wanted him to come under the influence of the moral atmosphere of that school. And, though that moral teaching was of an evangelical character, it in no way weakened the influence of his Catholic background, but rather deepened its essentially religious aspects. . . . How I wish that educators with your moral character, upright conscience, and profoundly Christian spirit could be multiplied in my country! "

Marcial Martinez de Ferrari has devoted his entire career to diplomacy after studying jurisprudence. He was secretary to the Chilean embassy in London for a number of years, and received an earned degree of Master of Laws from London University. Later he was Chilean Minister to Uruguay and Paraguay. His last appointment was that of ambassador to Brazil. Here are several sentences from his statement:

" It is with very special pleasure that I give this personal testimony of the high social, cultural, moral, and democratic influence of English and American missionaries and teachers in our America, an influence which is exerted all over the world without the pressure of dogmatism or a narrow ideology. . . . The example of so many missionaries who were true gentlemen and of lay teachers who were courageous and self-sacrificing, cannot but

[39] A Presbyterian mission school for boys in Santiago.

compel the praise and gratitude of every one whose heart beats with sincerity. The work of these missionaries inspires confidence because it is based on principles that are practical as well as idealistic.

" Chile knows how to judge with equanimity, and under the excellent guidance of her free and independent institutions she will extend, without any mental reservation or show of prejudice or intolerance, a most cordial welcome to the helpful co-operation of Protestant missions."

The dynamic and progressive president of the National University of Chile, Dr. Juvenal Hernandez, wrote:

" Chile is a land in which religious intolerance does not exist and where there is always a sincere respect for freedom of conscience. With pleasure we have looked upon those who have come to work among us, missionaries of different denominations. When they have faithfully preached their faith, honoring and respecting the country, society has freely offered its welcome to all of them. The work of evangelization among some groups of the working classes has made them more conscientious in the fulfillment of their duties, more sober, more disciplined in their home life, and more efficient as workers.

" When the schools sponsored by Protestant missions have not remained isolated, but have related themselves in a practical way to the cultural needs of the field in which they were established, they have accomplished a work which is worthy of every applause, because while teaching our youth, they have inculcated in them sentiments of brotherhood and true Pan-Americanism."

Chilean women are among the most progressive and emancipated in Latin America. Women enjoy the vote in municipal affairs, and several of them have served as mayors. Of the two Latin-American women who are in diplomatic service, one is a Chilean, Gabriela Mistral. One of Chile's leading women educators and writers is Señora Amanda Labarca, wife of the minister of education and well known in the United States where she has frequently appeared as a university lecturer. She is on the staff of the National University and a member of its council.

" I have witnessed," she writes in her statement to me, " the effect of Protestant teaching and the moral influence of Protestant missions among the popular classes of Chile. I am also well acquainted with the way in which the schools conducted by these missions have carried on their work without offending Catholic sentiment nor the family traditions of their pupils.

"The presence in Chile of these missionaries who have understood the Chilean spirit and the needs of our people, has greatly strengthened, without any doubt, a spirit of mutual understanding and affection between the United States from which they have come and our country.

"For these reasons and others which I might mention, I consider that the presence of these missionaries has been highly beneficial for our country and for our relations with the United States."

The Rotary movement has spread all over South America, but in no country has it developed so rapidly as in Chile. The president of the Santiago Club, one of the outstanding clubs in Rotary International, Mr. Luis Fontecilla, makes the following statement: "During many years I have worked in association with Protestants. I have found their integrity, their sobriety and honesty a very positive force for good in the industrial and agricultural activities of our country."

The name of Adolfo Ibañez, of Valparaíso, Chile, connotes sterling qualities. He is president of the Chilean Chamber of Commerce, and is well known in all South American republics as a business organizer. He was absent from Chile when I visited that country, but he later wrote, under date of November 30, 1943:

"On my return from Brazil I have had the painful surprise of learning of the inexplicable attack directed against the disinterested and most beneficial work of North American missionaries in our country. I can hardly believe that in this world where so much violence has been loosed, anyone should have dared attack the work, so humane and Christian, that you and your associates are carrying on. I hasten to send these hurried lines to you to encourage you to continue unflinchingly with your good work and to believe that it is gratefully appreciated by Chileans in all sectors of our society. Fortunately those of us who refuse to be blinded by fanaticism and prejudice are in the immense majority in Chile. The trouble is that five dissatisfied or enraged individuals make more noise than five thousand satisfied or appreciative persons who say nothing."

Dr. Hugo Fernandez Artucio, distinguished writer and member of the Uruguayan Legislature, had this to say of Protestant missions when I interviewed him:

"In no way do evangelical missions constitute an obstacle to the Good Neighbor policy. A Catholic mission would hardly be able to do the truly democratic and spiritual work which is done by the Protestant pastors and missionaries. Uruguay is a country that is free from control by the clergy and in which there is absolute freedom of religion. The Constitution of 1917 abolished the privileges which the Catholic Church once enjoyed over other religions and since then the official statement of our Constitution is that the state favors no one religion, but protects them all.

"The philosophic thought of this country is liberal. Our public schools are lay schools because the state is free from control by the clergy.

"The presence of Protestant missionaries in Uruguay has created a more favorable attitude toward the United States and brought about a better understanding between Uruguay and that country. Why? Protestant missionaries understand better than the Catholic missionaries the principles that are in line with the fundamental democratic spirit of the Uruguayan people. The evangelical missionaries have a profound sense of the ethical and social teachings of the New Testament. They adopt a much more sympathetic attitude toward the oppressed. This country is thoroughly committed to the idea of social justice. We are natural collaborators with those who preach social justice as an important part of their religious work.

"National unity will not be destroyed by the entrance of creeds and philosophies different from those of the Catholic church. One must not confuse unity with uniformity.

"Catholic representatives who might come from the United States would hardly be able to represent the United States which Uruguay respects and loves, because those missionaries from the

North American Catholic clergy would represent a religious organization of totalitarian character. The Catholicism that we have known has always denied the freedom of religion which President Roosevelt himself proclaimed and which presupposes not only the right to worship God according to one's conscience, but the right to publicly declare the convictions that one holds."

Dr. Américo Ghioldi, Buenos Aires editor and member of Congress, gave me the following statement:

"I am amazed at the question of whether the work of the Evangelical Church in Latin America is an obstacle to the Good Neighbor policy. . . . The work accomplished by English and American missionaries has caused no disturbance nor stirred up any incidents. The variety of their work — preaching, social service, educational recreation, solidarity with one's fellowmen, — is looked upon with sympathy by those of us who would like to see the social aspects of religion reunite men. As an educator, I cannot forget the contribution which a Protestant made to the development of education in my country when he introduced the Lancasterian method of teaching.

"On the other hand, the question which is under debate is really an anachronism. Is not the world fighting even now for religious liberty? Has not the whole world been horrorized by the consequences of religious totalitarianism?

"The world of today and the world of tomorrow will need tolerance and liberty of conscience. These are moral and practical necessities, because what system of doctrine can consider itself the sole and exclusive possessor of truth in all its variety?

"Unity in the midst of rich variety, presided over by liberty, is the aim of democracy and humanity. And it is as necessary to the latter as basal metabolism is to the physical life of the individual.

"We must allow the variety of human soils to produce their varied fruitage according to the nature of their beliefs!

"The jealousies generated in the stuffy atmosphere of the sacristies should not be allowed to blind our vision of the way!

"It is to be hoped that an understanding of the social evolution of America may help those exceedingly zealous persons who cause divisions, to understand also that a common root links Catholics and Protestants: The Bible. In the presence of that book jealousies and attitudes of intolerance ought to fade away."

Manuel Seoane, the Peruvian writer and journalist, who is also a Roman Catholic, was asked what his observation was of the work and influence of Protestantism in Spanish America.

"Protestant missions," he answered, "have carried out a quiet and tenacious effort of social service which compels our grateful recognition. Once when I was travelling in the Puno Mountain region of Peru where the Indians live in straw huts and under the most miserable and promiscuous conditions, I came upon a group of modest little houses, neatly painted, with ample windows for light and air, and a comfortable interior arrangement. They were built by Indians who had been evangelized and educated by Methodist missionaries who had gone to live among them in fulfilment of the Christian duty of helping one's fellow men. In Santiago, Chile, and in Buenos Aires, I have seen the effective work of the Salvation Army, which rescues the humbler classes from the influence of drink and which gives shelter to the homeless. These efforts have reacted on the Catholic circles, awakening them from their indifference and compelling them to undertake similar social activities.

"That is why it would be an inexcusable mistake to revive the Inquisition in the matter of granting passports. It would, besides, work untold damage to the Catholic Church itself by granting it a monopoly which is contrary to the nature of things and opposed to the religious needs of Latin America."

"Do you think that the Protestant Churches have a mission to fulfill in Latin America?" was my next question.

"Paradoxical as it may sound," he answered, "we need both Catholic priests and Protestant pastors. That will lead to an improvement in our religious life. It will provide us with the opportunity for comparison such as St. Augustine had before he finally chose the road he was to follow. What we want is to see something accomplished in the realm of the spirit, something more democratic and just, that would strengthen our moral life; something free from dead routine and a deadlier intransigence; something humanely religious which will co-operate with us in our fight against sensuality and ignorance, against selfishness and wickedness. That is: we demand a work of the spirit that will vivify in our midst the creative forces of Christianity."

Dr. Seoane mentions the effect of Protestant missionary effort on the Indians of Latin America. Many such testimonies may be garnered. In Mexico when the revolutionary leader, Benito Juárez, Zapotec Indian, came to power as president in 1857, he said Protestantism, because of the central place it gave the Bible, was "a religion which will compel the Indians to read." The Peruvian Congress, not long ago, paid tribute to this Indian work. One of its members, Dr. Efrain Trelles, said:

"I remind you of the work of the Protestant religion. The work accomplished by the Protestant missionaries in the provinces of Puno and Cuzco, is a highly praiseworthy service. It is a high honor for me to pay tribute today in the Parliament of Peru and do justice to that work. It is little known, but in my opinion it is the highest, the best and the noblest of its kind. It reaches the Indian very effectively and improves him especially along the line of spiritual things. I have had the satisfaction of discovering that these Indians were being taught the fundamental rudiments of hygiene and medicine. Furthermore they had acquired something which other Indians, who had not been reached by these missionaries, had not yet achieved and which Catholicism has not given them: a strengthened personality and an awakened spirit." [40]

I called on the leader of the Socialist Party of Uruguay, Dr. José Pedro Cardoso. He is the leading nerve specialist of that country. I asked him how Roman Catholic Uruguay was.

"There is a liberal and anti-clerical tradition in Uruguay which shows no signs of weakening," was his answer. "The *Batlle* political party which is the strongest in Uruguay, has had a most radical social program and a bitter anti-Catholic bias. In the course of these latter years it has greatly modified its extremely radical social principles; but its anti-Catholic fervor is as strong as ever."

I asked him if he thought that the presence of Protestant mis-

[40] See *Journal of Debates of the Constitutional Congress*. Lima, Peru, 1931.

sionaries in Uruguay was an offense to the people of that country.

He laughed at the idea. " On the contrary," he said, " we feel that democratic Protestantism is, after all, fighting for the same things that we fight for. We are greatly alarmed at the political influence which the Roman Catholic Church exerts in the United States."

In my visit to Dr. Cardoso I was accompanied by an American Protestant missionary, Mr. Earl Smith, who runs a Good Will Industry and city mission in what could be called the stockyards district of Montevideo. When Smith expressed a desire to become a member of the Socialist Party of Uruguay, he found that they had a rule against the admittance of clergymen to the party! So a special party convention was held, and the rule was changed!

José Pedro Varela is rector, or president, as we would say, of the National University of Montevideo. His is a name weighted with great cultural traditions. He is the grandson of the original José Pedro Varela, famous poet and writer, the Horace Mann of Uruguay.

" I am a liberal," he said to me. " It is to be regretted that liberalism in Uruguay has been, until recently, identified with a bitter opposition, not only to clericalism but to religious faith itself. It was a natural but unfortunate reaction to the long period of Catholic domination in the early decades of our independence. I am opposed to clericalism but not to religion. I try to be fair and impartial. One of my professors, a brilliant young man, is a Roman Catholic. He refused to identify himself with the *Union Civica* (the Catholic party) and he publicly rebuked his fellow-Catholics for entering politics as a religious body."

I asked Dr. Varela if he thought missionaries were an obstacle to the Good Neighbor policy.

" They are not," was his answer, and he pointed out that these representatives of North American religious life had done much to destroy the legend that the United States was completely materialistic. " Furthermore," he added, " we are very proud of the fact that our Constitution stands for religious freedom, and we are resentful of any effort to annul this liberal attitude."

I was very much interested in his final statement.

"When I was a university student," he said, "you could count on the fingers of both hands the number of students who professed to be Roman Catholics. I am discovering a great change today in this matter. The Catholic element is growing among the students and today there is a considerable group that is openly Catholic and that is organized as such. These students have occasionally used our assembly hall for lectures under their auspices."

Thirty-odd years ago a group of brilliant and courageous university men organized themselves in Uruguay for the purpose of leading their country toward the liberal ideas which came from France, Great Britain, and the United States. To these students, who later became poets, journalists, and statesmen, Uruguay owes much of the amazing progress which has put it culturally at the head of the Latin-American nations. One of this creative group is Dr. Manuel Nuñez Regueiro, at present Uruguayan consul in the important river port of Rosario in Argentina. He is dean of the consular corps of that city and professor of philosophy in the National University of Rosario; honorary associate of the Institute of Ancient and Medieval History of the University of Buenos Aires; corresponding member of the Brazilian Institute of Coimbra, and president of the Learned Society of Rosario. All these activities and his consular duties have not been able to keep his vigorous pen idle. He is author of an impressive list of books.[41]

"Has your experience been such as to permit you to evaluate the influence of Protestantism in the countries on both sides of the River Plate?" was one of the first questions I put to him.

"I have been in contact with Protestantism from early childhood. In Montevideo (where I was born) I have been able to appreciate its healthful influence as one of the most precious of spiritual treasures, projecting itself into the life of the youth of the land. Out of the Sunday Schools came men the memory of whom stirs us. They ennobled an era which flourished morally as well as

[41] *Suma Contra una Nueva Edad Media; Conocimiento y Creencia; La Honda Inquietud; Fundamentos de la Anterosofía; Anterosofía Racional; De Nuevo Habló Jesús; Filosofía Integral,* etc. Editorial y Librería Ruiz, Córdoba 1281, Rosario, Argentina.

spiritually. The early knowledge of the Bible has penetrated deeply into the heart of the young people, and they have enlisted in Christ's invisible army. From among them were recruited some of the best citizens of our country, who placed themselves at the service of their native land and humanity. I have observed the same phenomenon in Argentina. The leaven of the Gospel transforms character for the better, and is the best guarantee and recommendation of the moral life of the citizen. These peoples of the River Plate region, left to themselves, and subject to the influence of the ' Catholic Action,' had been educated in the dogmatism of authoritarianism, which discounted reason. Consequently intolerance and fanaticism were developed in them. They became hostile to all liberal social practices. Protestantism has freed us from these dangers, with its liberal teachings based on the living testimony of the law of the Gospel which makes men free. Some defenders of the orthodoxy of the Church, who condemn Descartes for having proclaimed the right to freedom of thought as over against the authority of Aristotle, still maintain with Thomas Aquinas that the State should not permit the existence of certain religious confessions and that heretics should be punished. In the Americas, Protestantism has freed us from this fear also, thank God."

" What is the fundamental difference which you have observed between Protestantism and Catholicism, with regard to their influence in South American countries? " I then asked Dr. Nuñez Regueiro.

" Protestantism is a living religion, thanks to its interest in reading and meditating constantly on the teachings of the Bible, a family book with much that can reach the understanding of a child. Protestantism is a life, not a formula. Catholicism is more often a formula, rather than a life. Its dry, soulless formality is characterized by ritualism. It emphasizes the externals of life. There is no true vital content. Protestantism knows and maintains that ' it is better to obey God than men.' To safeguard this article of faith, it is willing to suffer all sorts of adversity, if only it may please God. The wholesome influence of this behavior is revealed in our River Plate countries wherever Protestantism has influenced public and private life. If religion is the effectual ' union of the soul with God,' it finds, for its proper manifestation, a freer and more propitious atmosphere within Protestantism than within a purely formulist and dogmatic Catholicism which counsels tithes and first-fruits for the Church but denies salvation to all outside the Church of Rome. The Catholic lives more in harmony with the *visible* Church; the Protestant, more in agreement with the *invisible* Church, the invisible Body of Jesus Christ, in which all may be saved, Catholics, Protestants, Jews, Mohammedans, Buddhists, barbarians, Scythians, if only they will do the will of God."

One of Argentina's leading woman educators is Dr. Angela Santa Cruz. For many years she was principal of the only girls' secondary school in Buenos Aires. She has now retired from active teaching and is giving her time to religious work through the local Young Women's Christian Association. She received me in her home. Very soon we were on the subject of religion. She had felt the urge to find an expression of religious faith that would be intellectually respectable. The experience of this cultured woman is typical of the many pilgrim souls in Latin America who have launched out in eager quest for truth and light. She has not gone to the confessional since the days of her young womanhood, nor has she partaken of the Eucharist.

Here is the story of her spiritual pilgrimage as told to me:

"I was born into a Catholic family and was made to observe the religious precepts of that Church. And I have continued as an adherent of that Church, partly as a result of the force of tradition and sentimental reasons, and partly because of the need which we all have for spiritual food.

"My later studies in philosophy, history, literature, together with my reading and my knowledge of life and of people, gave me a broadening conception of religion. I continue to consider myself linked to the Catholic Church, which I attend from time to time. I hear and judge with my own reasoning the most authoritative spokesmen of the Church, especially when they are dealing with subjects relating to the social order, because I believe that in this day and age the teaching of Christ applied to personal life and to the life of the community is the only force capable of saving humanity. Contact with men and women of other branches of

Christianity has given me the opportunity to appreciate the valuable influence of their work in the field of spiritual culture.

" I have visited conventions of Methodist women; I have often listened to the preaching of Protestant pastors; I maintain a close friendship with the deaconess of the Protestant Church in my native town; in company with Catholic friends I have attended a spiritual retreat organized by members of other churches. In one of them I heard the inspired voice of Susanna Dietrich; I know the philanthropic work done by the great Mr. Morris, which is the admiration of all. I know of many schools and cultural centers which are doing a highly constructive piece of work and exerting a valuable Christian influence. All of this enables me to affirm with all sincerity that they constitute a moral and spiritual force of great importance for the development of our country." [42]

The Chilean writer and member of one of the leading Roman Catholic families of Chile, Dr. Benjamín Subercaseaux, was invited in 1943 to the United States as a guest of honor by Washington. While here he commented on the campaign of the American hierarchy against Protestant missions in Latin America, as follows:

" I believe that too much importance is being given to the protest against the activities of the Protestants in our countries. We in Latin America have duly appreciated and recognized the value of their work, particularly in social affairs, and in no instance have they endangered the stability of our Catholic faith. On the contrary, they have alleviated both the physical and spiritual needs of the masses and have helped to give impetus and strength to the somewhat feeble activities of some Catholic groups. Besides this, the Constitutions of our countries, being openly democratic, have never exerted official pressure to stop Protestants from acting freely in South America. Any inclination of our governments to limit the freedom of any religious sect would be very unfavorably viewed and would raise a storm of protest." [43]

[42] For complete statement, see Appendix I.

[43] For a full statement, written in March, 1943, by Dr. Subercaseaux on this subject, see " Protestant Missions in South America," in *The Pan American*, June, 1944.

The legend of South American resentment against Protestant missions still persists. But it is increasingly hard for its supporters to make a case. The denial of any such resentment is coming from the Latin Americans themselves. It is the achievements of Protestantism in social and educational service which prompted Dr. Elio, until recently Foreign Minister of Bolivia, to say to Allen Haden, Latin-American correspondent of *The Chicago Daily News*, " We welcome Christian missions — not only Catholic ones — to colonize our Indians whom we have neglected."

In 1940 an American corporation tried to buy up all the Bolivian wolfram for $17 a unit. A few days later, a Japanese commercial commission offered $27. After impassioned discussions in the Bolivian press and Congress, the wolfram was sold to the American Company for $23. It was this incident which led Luis Alberto Sánchez, in his book *Un Sudamericano en Norteamerica* [44] (a South American in North America), to say: " The Good Neighbor policy has not altered the mentality of North American business men. . . . It is still far from the heart and mind of the financiers and people of the United States."

Protestant missionaries in Latin America exemplified the Good Neighbor policy long before it was conceived in Washington. It was not bigotry nor any spirit of aggression or imperialism which led them there. It was the same spirit of disinterested service which Madame Chiang Kai-shek praised when she said: " For the last two hundred years you have been sending all kinds of people and organizations to China. But only one came with no intention of getting anything out of China and that was the Christian Church."

[44] Ercilla, Santiago, Chile, 1943.

VII: Religious Uniformity and National Unity

TWENTY YEARS AGO AN ATTEMPT WAS MADE TO DISCREDIT PROT-
estantism in Latin America with the argument that it was the advance agent of American imperialism. Today that accusation
would fall on indifferent ears. So a new line of attack has had to
be devised, and the hierarchy has found it in the thesis, sedulously spread all over the southern republics, that national unity
will never be achieved without religious uniformity. That is to
say, in order to have a strong, united country, everyone must belong to the same Church.

One meets this idea frequently. It appears as one of the arguments against Protestantism in the pastoral letter issued by the
archbishops and bishops of Peru in 1943: "There is no binding
agent so strong as religion for harmonizing wills and uniting
hearts. . . . But on the other hand there is no more corrosive
solvent than diversity of creed for disuniting the members of a
community."

This is the medieval theory that religious solidarity is essential
to the stability of the civil community. As used by the hierarchy
in Latin America and the United States it is a subtle appeal to
patriotism. It is one of the main pivots of the *Hispanidad* movement. We have heard it frequently put in this way: To be a good
Brazilian, Argentine, or Mexican, you must be a Roman Catholic.
What is the response of thoughtful Latin Americans to this propaganda? Dr. Manuel Núñez Regueiro, whom I quoted in the pre-
ceding chapter, has this to say about it:

"True national unity does not come from the letter, but rather
is the result of the holy, patriotic spirit on which it feeds. And
this spirit is the spirit of love, understanding, liberty, tolerance,
and respect for law. Everyone who professes the golden rule, and
practices it as far as possible, loving God above all things, and
loving his neighbor as himself, labors by deed and example toward
the attainment of true, authentic national unity. Without God the

91

highest values in life will not be achieved. The religious idea and the supreme value of holiness are not the exclusive property of any church or religion. Nothing is more lamentable than religious intolerance. We in Latin America know its fateful consequences. The knowledge of the truth makes us truly free, as the Gospel states, and that truth cannot be the exclusive property of any church, Catholic, Protestant or Jewish. 'In the light of reason,' says Edgar S. Brightman, 'no nation, race or tongue, no philosophy, no religion can claim a monopoly on truth and values.' National unity will be strong where true freedom of thought, of opinion and of religious creed prevail. It will flourish in an atmosphere of peace, fraternity and tolerance. Catholic intolerance, proscribing or hindering the worship of other religions, will never favor national unity. We have seen the excellent fruits of the other policy, of our friends the Protestants in the great nation to the north, which had liberty as its norm. Faced with the enemies of freedom, we must be on guard that the darkness of medievalism may not fall upon the New World."

Dr. Helio Lobo, the distinguished Brazilian statesman and writer, when asked what he thought of the suggestion that national stability depended on religious uniformity, answered:

"That is an absurd argument. The unity of a country depends upon the diversity of its economic, cultural and even religious life. By what I have been able to observe in other countries, Catholicism prospers when it has Protestantism as a stimulus. The Protestant pulpit constantly exerts its influence in favor of liberty. No greater national unity or civic zeal will be found anywhere than in Switzerland, Holland, Canada and the United States, — all countries in which religious belief is divided."

"Should South America be declared a closed continent?" we then asked him.

"Certainly not. It would offend the liberal sentiment of Brazil. Discrimination against religious beliefs such as we have witnessed in other countries, has always been repugnant to us. We would not tolerate any such thing in our country."

Dr. Manuel Carlos Ferraz, president of the Brazilian Court of Appeals, gave it as his opinion that there was no reason to fear that Protestant propaganda would weaken the political unity of Brazil. "There are countries," he said, "of solid national unity whose population professes a variety of creeds; Switzerland, Holland, Canada, Prussia, and even France are examples. On the other hand there are Catholic countries whose national unity is weak, as in Spain, which is a country torn by internal dissension; Italy, whose lack of national cohesion explains, in large part, its misfortunes; Central America, — Catholic and divided into a number of small republics. There does not seem to be any necessary relation between national cohesion and the creed professed by the majority. And if there were, then the facts would favor the Protestant countries where a great and more perfect political unity exists. Incidentally, there is no doubt that in the present war Catholic countries reveal a notable weakness in their spirit of resistance and combativeness, due, no doubt, to their internal divergencies."

Dr. Francisco Venancio Filho is one of Brazil's outstanding educators. He is ex-president of the Brazilian Educational Association and professor of the University of Brazil. In answer to my questions, he gave me the following statement:

"The suggestion that South America should become a closed continent to every faith except Roman Catholicism is absurd. First of all it would be proof of an intolerance that is incompatible with the degree of civilization which we have achieved. Then it would carry us back to a period previous to our Constitution of 1824 which established religious tolerance. In a free country, religious freedom will be a point of social honor. In mutual respect for the convictions of others, based on the sincerity with which each professes his faith, lies the great Christian teaching of universal brotherhood. I do not agree that national unity can be secured through coercive measures. Our bonds of national unity are strong enough to make it unnecessary to have recourse to odious measures of intolerance. If it be true that in the colonial period, due to certain historical circumstances, the Catholic Church was a factor favorable to Brazilian unity, it is absolutely unnecessary in our day to try and strengthen this unity by limiting the freedom with which other religious faiths would function."

While his consulting room was gradually filling with patients, I hurriedly interviewed Dr. Moacyr E. Alvaro, of São Paulo, the best-known oculist in Brazil. He is a Fellow of the American Academy of Ophthalmology and Otolaryngology; he has frequently been a delegate from Brazil to scientific conferences in the United States. He has on several occasions lectured before the Medical Associations of the United States. Young, brilliant, polished and with a perfect command of the English language, he responded generously to my questioning. I give only a few short sentences from my copious notes: "American missionaries are welcome in Brazil. Rather than ask whether the people who come to Brazil are Catholic or Protestant, we should be more interested in knowing if they are Christian. Christian morality is the foundation of both Catholicism and Protestantism. National unity exists in Switzerland and the United States where there is a diversity of religions; Catholicism is dominant and other religions are practically non-existent in Spain and yet that country is the most politically disunited country in the world. Catholics in the United States are in a minority and minorities are always resentful. The moral influence of Protestantism on the working classes of Brazil is notable; I have seen a spirit of dignity and self-respect awakened in the Negro people and Indians of this country. Protestant culture has an important contribution to make to Brazil, — this does not mean that I wish Brazil to become Protestant. With the spread of education, Roman Catholic methods will have to change."

Colombia is justly proud of its fine, new public library building in Bogotá. The man at the head of this institution is characterized by a vigor of expression, an originality of character and brilliance of mind that makes him stand out as one of Colombia's unique intellectuals. I found Dr. Enrique Uribe White in his office in the library, with his pipe and his books, — two adjuncts from which he is inseparable! On the subject of religious monopoly or uniformity he had this to say:

"It does not seem to me that the governments of these republics should yield to the pressure being brought to bear by the Catholic hierarchies for the purpose of obtaining a virtual monopoly in control over the souls of men. This converting of Latin

America into a religious 'closed shop' would only revive in the age of bombing planes the old fanaticism of the Inquisitors, the Calvinists and the Puritans. Neither do I consider it desirable from a cultural standpoint, since every proclamation of a new doctrine, every new interpretation of dogmas or beliefs are movements of the mind that lead to free examination, to reading and to the awakening of the spirit. And it seems to me that one merchandise that is urgently needed in this land, is that of ideas, whatever the wrapping in which they come. *It is time that the breezes of the Reformation which have delayed so many centuries in crossing the Atlantic, should blow this way* [italics ours]. Some sections of our countries still struggle along lines of the sixteenth century." [45]

When Colombia took over its educational system, freeing it from the control of the clergy, part of the ambitious plans for the new, modern system was a new national university. A magnificent property has been secured on the outskirts of Bogotá and a plan has been outlined which when completed will give Colombia one of the finest campuses and the most imposing group of buildings in the whole of Latin America. A number of the buildings are already constructed and classes are functioning on the new campus.

The rector, as university presidents are called in Latin America, Dr. Julio Carrizosa Valenzuela, received the writer with the unfailing courtesy that distinguishes Colombians.

" I have never heard of any difficulties being created for good inter-American relations by the presence of missionaries in our country," he said. " You will find two kinds of Catholics in our country. There is the simple and rather fanatical type of Catholicism of the country people. Then there is the educated Catholic whom you will find friendly and liberal. I am a Catholic. My family dates back to colonial days and has always been staunchly Roman Catholic. I practice my religion and deeply love it. But I do not see that it should in any way offend us to have the representatives of other religious faiths come to our country. Of course, the clergy will always resent the presence of other faiths. But I cannot see that they have any intelligent reason for doing so.

[45] For complete statement, see Appendix K.

After all, these Protestant missionaries do not come preaching atheism or practicing immoralities. The important thing is the moral conduct of these missionaries. They come preaching a religion of virtue and self-control. And that is all to the good. The priests themselves should be grateful for the example of virtue and righteous living which Protestants are giving the country. I cannot imagine why the presence of Protestant missionaries in Colombia should in any way mar relations between the two countries. At least, the missionary activity of the United States will prove to the people of this country that, far from being the country of the 'almighty dollar,' the United States is a profoundly religious country."

I thanked this distinguished educator and apologized for taking so much of his time. " I am glad you came," he said as he accompanied me to the door; " we have talked on religious matters, — a subject which very seldom comes up for discussion in our country. Come again! "

National unity can never be secured by compulsion. It can never be secured by the imposition of an outward code of conduct which gives only a false appearance of national unity. Diversity of opinion is not inimical to true unity. Truth emerges from the clash of opposite judgments or of opposing opinions. There can be no democracy without opposition and free criticism. Opposition is an indispensable element for real unity or collaboration. It is as important as one's adversary in a game; there would be no game without an opponent . . . unless you prefer solitaire!

National unity is further endangered when a religious body takes on the character of a political organization. In South America the Roman Catholic Church has had three centuries of untrammeled opportunity for the creation of a united people. But what are the facts? Continental solidarity among the southern republics as well as national unity is still a far-off dream. The precarious condition of relations between some of our Latin American neighbors is revealed by the following cablegram of the United Press to American newspapers:

" Press reports from Costa Rica today indicated the possibility of a diplomatic crisis between Costa Rica and Guatemala. The rising tension came out of Guatemala's refusal to permit entry of Costa Rica's Archbishop Msgr. Victor Sanabria to attend the eucharistic congress at Guatemala City. The Guatemalan press charged that Sanabria was 'Communist.'" Can you imagine the present United States Government refusing a passport to any Roman Catholic archbishop?

Are the Americas to the south united? Let the distinguished Peruvian author, Dr. Luis Alberto Sánchez, at present lecturing in several American universities, answer: [46]

"If there is one thing that we lack it is an affirmative spiritual unity. Having grown up in a dogmatic atmosphere which has bred in us the habit of closed affirmations and final negations, we lack that inner fire which reveals the presence of a true faith. Faith and dogma have never been synonymous. The former is life itself; the latter is its crystallization. Between the two, history develops. Faith is tireless and creative; dogma is finally static. We, in Latin America, are united in our scepticism and negation, because we have always lived under the sign of monopoly: economic during the colonial period, political during the earlier independence period, financial later on and clerical all the time. Our Catholics, who constitute the immense majority on our continent, are poor at the practice of their beliefs because they lack that inner fire which is the result of a deep and sincere faith. This element of faith is absent because our people never discuss their spiritual problems; they are told what to believe; they never elaborate or work out their beliefs. That is why contact with other creeds could serve as a stimulus to a real faith. Why is it that Catholics in the United States have a higher and more constructive sense of their religion and of life? For the reason that they live face to face with a vigorous and watchful Protestant Church. Why is it that Protestants in Latin America are nearly always exemplary? Because they live under the shadow of a powerful Catholic Church."

Dr. Sánchez then gives us his reasons why he does not wish South America to become a " closed continent " religiously.

"In order to find itself, our spiritual unity needs to feel the challenge of thoughts and attitudes that will be different from

[46] For complete statement, see Appendix F.

ours, thoughts and attitudes that will be the outcome of a powerful inner force. So shall we learn how to argue without aggression, how to compare without producing schism, how to go deeply
into things without digging graves. The root of our one-sidedness
must be dug up. The selfish sources of monopoly must be dried
up, and the springs of tolerance and free discussion deepened. . . ."

Out of his own deep experience, Dr. Sánchez finally concludes:

" Fundamentally a believing people though temporarily sceptical and consequently filled with uncertainty, Latin Americans
need to find their way by looking up, by taking their bearings and
examining different routes. My own experience has taught me that
this slow and painful method, this wading through layers of patient routine, is the best way of getting at the essence of things.
Let people from everywhere come to our countries; let them come
each with his truth, his culture, his language, his religion. Here,
with us, they will be converted to what is ours in the measure to
which what is ours is purified and amplified in contact with what
is theirs. Our great weakness, I repeat, is that of living colonially
and of being treated as colonials. We do not need liberators whose
first word to us would be one learned in some foreign government office, however generous or righteous that word might be.
Let religious faith come to us without the trappings of monopoly
and without the rubrications of imperial privilege. Faith is not
created nor strengthened by external methods. It is an intimate
process, an unsettling process, an eminently personal process. It
is generated as the result of an irresistible necessity and it develops best in open spaces, in contact with other lives, other ideas
and above all in contact with nature which though close to man is
still so foreign to man.

" Let no government office, therefore, pretend to take us under
its tutelage even in matters religious. Let them leave us free to
determine at least our own metaphysical destiny, since they have
deprived us of the privilege of doing this with our material existence. And may they believe us when we say that there are areas
in individual and collective life where the worst prescription . . .

is a prescription! And the problem we have been considering is a case in point."

What are we to think of the quality of a people whose national unity is disturbed by differing religious faiths? Very aptly the distinguished Argentine Roman Catholic educator, Dr. Casal Castel, in his written statement to me says:

" If other religious faiths were a menace to our personality, we should have to confess that our national unity was a very tenuous affair. If our spiritual cohesion is solid and sure, our national unity and solidarity will be able to meet the challenge of other currents of thought. Besides this, I do not believe that the different branches of Christianity within a Catholic country should be considered enemies, because if that country is really Catholic, it will be characterized by a Christian universality."

National unity in and between the several countries of Latin America will be difficult to achieve as long as the Roman Catholic Church continues to play politics. As long as it remains monopolistic, authoritarian and consequently antiliberal and antidemocratic, *it will be a divisive influence.*

VIII: Latin America Needs a Religious Revolution

BETWEEN RELIGION AND LIFE IN LATIN AMERICA AN ALMOST BOT-
tomless chasm yawns. Until recently no one could be a member
of the powerful Socialist party in Argentina who belonged to a
Church. A few years ago a brilliant woman leader of this party
was expelled from the organization because in a public address
she had dared to refer to Jesus Christ, and to suggest that his
principles were supremely important for the building of society.
These industrial classes in Latin America have swung away from
a religion which appears to them to be exclusively a matter of
dogma and ceremony, a religion motivated by the idea that, if you
say the right prayer to the right god, he will get you out of all
your troubles!

Not only the working classes, but the intellectuals also need to
be saved from dilettantism, from superficiality, from cynicism.
Young men in South America grow old too soon. Idealism is hard
to achieve, hard to maintain, and easy to lose. The educated
classes need a faith.

South America is a continent in need of an ethic. It needs to
learn that a religious man should be a good man; that, as Professor Coe says, "the true meaning of the Church is more righteous-
ness in the community, its introverted meaning is more Church."
It is a continent in need of a faith — not faith as mental acquies-
cence, but as personal adherence; faith defined as the Protestant
tradition usually interprets it: as commitment to the Christian
way of life and personal allegiance to its Founder, Jesus Christ.

The corruption of the best is the worst. No Christianity is
"good enough" for any people, if it is not the Christianity of
Jesus Christ. A corrupted or spurious Christianity, in our country
or any country, is the greatest threat of all. No atheist or heretic
can equal the harm done by a sham Christian. The second best is
often the most dangerous enemy of the best of all. The traditional
Christianity of South America has produced its saints. In an elite

100

group a high spiritual level has been reached. But in the masses, where indifference has not alienated them completely from the Roman Catholic Church, you will find an outward mechanical consent given to the teaching of the clergy, but little inward fealty to or love for the religion they profess.

Dr. Julio Navarro Monzó, the well-known Argentine writer, once defined religion as "a profound sentiment, an intimate experience, a reality in itself, which coolly sends a Francis Xavier to die in Asia, a Livingstone to evangelize the heart of Africa, a Florence Nightingale to succor the wounded on the battlefields of Crimea." [47] An admirable definition; but if that is religion, there is very little of it in the southern continent and perhaps too little in this northern continent!

In the closing evening of the international student conference held by the Y.M.C.A. in Uruguay, one law student voiced the sentiment of many by saying:

"Men, I have a confession to make. When my fellow students asked me to represent them at this camp I declined in anger at the thought that they should consider me willing to attend a meeting held under religious auspices. They pressed the invitation a third time before I accepted. My father and mother have always fought religion, and I have thought it my patriotic duty to do what I could against religion in my country. But I must confess that I never heard of religion as you men interpreted it — something inside a man which makes him happy and useful. This has opened up to me a new world." Here was a young South American who had discovered the difference between religion as magic and religion as moral power.

Protestantism has brought a breath of new spiritual life to Latin America. It is interpreting Christianity in a new way to people who have thought it their "patriotic duty to do what they could against religion."

"It is time that the winds of the Reformation reached our lands. They have delayed too long. We need them to blow through some sections of our countries that still struggle along lines of

[47] *The Religious Problem in Latin American Culture.* Continental Y.M.C.A., Montevideo, Uruguay, 1925.

the sixteenth century," so said Dr. Enrique Uribe White, director of the National Library of Bogotá, Colombia, in my interview with him.

Why did the winds of the Reformation not reach our shores? Why are the Latin countries still struggling to overcome a profound religious lag?

While the struggle of a century to found and build up a real democracy has been Latin America's great problem, its still greater tragedy is the fact that the leaders of these peoples have never been conscious of the moral and religious aspect of the undertaking.

Are the Latins capable of democracy? Charles Maurras thinks that they are not. Are we sure, he would ask us, that democracy is not an exclusive product of the Anglo-Saxon mind, and therefore incompatible with the Latin character? Can we prove that democracy and good government have ever gone hand in hand in Latin countries? Maurras thinks that we cannot. His ideal would be a return to that creation of the Renaissance: the absolute monarchy.

One has to recognize that in the Latin countries of Europe and America, political institutions are very largely a servile copy of Anglo-Saxon models. A constitutional monarchy in Spain or Italy, the republic in France or Portugal, the federal government in Brazil or Argentina, are only imitations, and poor at that, of the constitutions of Great Britain and the United States. As we look at the history of the governments of these countries, it is hard not to be pessimistic about the capacity of the Latins for a democratic type of life or government. This feeling will, in part, explain the wave of antidemocratic reaction which has recently spread over Latin America.

But Maurras is mistaken when he claims to find in the absolute monarchy the highest point in the history of the Latin peoples. The truth is that there were expressions of the democratic spirit among Latin peoples just as old as any that we might cite among the Anglo-Saxons.

The earliest expressions of democracy appear in Spain and Italy during the Middle Ages. As far back as the seventh century in Spain, the *Fuero Juzgo* stated the principle that " the peoples were not made for kings but kings for the peoples, nor did the kings create the peoples, but the peoples made them kings." While the barons in England were presenting their demands which formed the basis of the Magna Charta of Anglo-Saxon liberties, the nobles and bourgeoisie of Aragon, meeting in Tarragona, faced Peter III, invoking that ancient tradition of privileges and liberties which went back even to the time of the Goths. Thus were guaranteed the celebrated privileges which the succeeding monarch, Alfonso III, the liberal, was compelled to sanction in 1287. Spaniards recall with justifiable pride the formula with which the representatives of Aragon met to swear fealty to the new king: "We who are worth as much as thou, make thee our king and master, provided that thou dost respect our rights and liberties, and if not, no."

If this is true, then the fact that the Spanish American peoples are slavishly copying Anglo-Saxon institutions does not prove that they are unfit for democratic institutions, but it simply signifies that the Anglo-Saxons were able to carry forward and expand a movement which the Latins were not able to continue for reasons which it may be worth-while to analyze.

Why is it that the Anglo-Saxon peoples could continue strengthening their liberties until democracy was definitely established in their world?

The Latins and the Anglo-Saxons have followed two different traditions whose synthesis has never been as yet accomplished. The one is the Greco-Roman classic tradition. The other, which has been the prolific mother of every romantic movement that the world has seen, is the Hebrew-Christian tradition. The Latins have kept closer to the Greco-Roman while the Anglo-Saxons have followed the Hebrew-Christian tradition.

The democracies of the Middle Ages, like every democracy, were the product of Christianity. The classic tradition made no contribution. Democracy did not exist in the Greek republics. They were true aristocracies or oligarchies, composed of a minority that exercised authority over a great mass of slaves on whose labor that handful of citizens lived. Even less democracy can be found in the imperial tradition of Rome.

Democracy has existed, and can exist, only among men who believe in but one God, the common Father of the human race, and who believe, therefore, in human equality and fraternity. A political democracy has never yet appeared outside of the bounds of Christianity nor will it prosper where "personal religion" is unknown.

The seed of Christianity fell among the Latin peoples of Europe and, with the development of this new spiritual leaven, a movement toward democracy was started. Then came the Renaissance with the powerful resurrection of interest in the Greco-Roman pagan culture and ideals. The pagan aspects of the Renaissance never reached the northern countries of Europe with very much strength. But southern Europe fell under the spell of the new culture. It must be remembered that this ancient paganism never entirely disappeared in the Latin countries. There are found poets who sang its praise and sculptors who glorified it in marble. No such enthusiasm was felt in the northern countries for the pagan aspects of the Renaissance, hence it never took such deep root. The Renaissance had the tragic effect in the Latin countries of killing the incipient movement toward democracy which Christianity had started.

The influence of the Renaissance was political as well as moral. With the discovery of the *Pandects in Amalfi,* a deepened interest was aroused in the study of Roman law. At that time the struggle between the king and the feudal lords was being intensified. We can understand how the former welcomed the old Roman principle that "*whatever pleases the Prince, shall have the force of law.*" The doctrine of the divine right of kings began to occupy the center of the stage. Universities were founded for the purpose of teaching the newly discovered principles. Thus some of the old universities of Spain became bulwarks of absolutism. Much of the political organization of those days, Christian and democratic in its principles and origins, began to yield to the influence of Caesarism.

In the northern countries, where the pagan aspects of the Renaissance had not been made so attractive, Christianity was able to continue its quiet work. Thus the Reformation appeared, and we must not forget that, just as the Renaissance meant the coming to life of the old paganism, so part of the deep significance of the Protestant Reformation lies in the fact that it was a strong protest against the pagan elements that were so powerfully leavening life in the countries of southern Europe.

As a reaction against this pagan tendency of their day, some great spiritual personalities appeared in the Latin countries. In Spain, Saint Teresa and Saint John of the Cross represent the mystical tradition which tried to accomplish in the south what the Protestant Reformation was achieving in the north. Later this spiritual tradition was continued in France by such great preachers as Fénelon and Pascal.

The trouble with Latin America is that neither the saving influence of these great Latin mystics nor the invigorating breezes of the Reformation ever reached its lands. Only the spirit of the Renaissance, the materialism and vanity of a superficial culture, reached South America. This dark picture, of course, is relieved by some shining personalities: Bartolome de las Casas, Francisco Solano, and others who came to Latin America with true apostolic devotion. But the vast majority of those who landed on the shores of the southern continent were dominated by the sensual pagan influences of the Renaissance.

The settlement of the continents of North and South America assumed widely divergent patterns. An editorial which appeared in the Buenos Aires great daily, *La Prensa*, while I was in that city in October, 1943, summarizes these two different historical trends and interprets them. The fact that the editorial is Latin-American and was written at a time when a dictatorial and reactionary government was suppressing freedom and proposing to enforce the teaching of Roman Catholicism in the public schools increases its significant bearing on our problems:

"Let it not be forgotten that the stream of immigration that flowed toward the northern continent was largely spontaneous. In lands that fell to the Spanish crown immigration was of a totally different sort. To North America went groups of settlers who on their own initiative left their native lands seeking freedom, and above all freedom of conscience. . . . For all who came to the new lands there was freedom of work and freedom of conscience, full and equal individual rights for all. . . .

" Here on our continent, on the other hand, a different system was established and very diverse also were the effects of three centuries spent under the authority of the mother country. Absolutism characterized the government. . . . Everything that was fundamental was kept under the control of the sovereign with the advice of the Crown Councils. Immigration was limited only to those of Hispanic origin and those who professed the religious faith which not only dominated the Spanish peninsula but which excluded all other faiths. . . . Education was so completely neglected by the government that at the commencement of the 19th century the number of literates among the population was very scarce.

" The influence of all these adverse factors weighed heavily in our slow and painful social and economic evolution, which never went very far beyond the most rudimentary conditions. Thus poorly equipped were we on the eve of our struggle for independence. We suddenly found ourselves possessed of an immense territory with only one inhabitant to every seven square miles! At that same period, however, the inhabitants of the United States were over seven millions and their influence on world affairs, due to their power and culture, was an accomplished fact.

" There we have the patent results of two different policies; the one held liberty as its norm, the other exercised its greatest zeal in suffocating the most elemental manifestations of liberty."

Here in a nutshell you have a penetrating analysis of the problem of Latin America. It is the problem of a bad start, politically, economically, and morally. I have transcribed parts of this editorial, for it is my desire in this book to let Latin Americans themselves express their views and convictions.

Another Latin-American statement of the disparity between North and South which emphasizes the religious variance was called to my attention by a friend in Montevideo, Uruguay. It is from a copy of *America*, a liberal magazine published in Havana, Cuba. It says in part: " In the formation of every country certain moral principles and factors enter into play . . . and these determine the life and affect the progress of those countries. And is there, perchance, a more powerful moral factor than religion in the shaping of social life? . . . As the history of the Americas has developed in two different ways, so there are two different types of Christianity in the new world. Anglo-America is a child of the Reformation: Latin America is the product of Catholic sculpturing. In both sections of the New World the democratic system of government was established and it is easy to trace the effect on each of the different types of religion under which it developed.

" The thirteen American colonies were founded by pilgrims who fled from religious and political intolerance and who reached the shores of America with the purpose of establishing a new society based on respect and liberty for man. Their first governments were pure democracies and a very significant detail is the fact that the first assemblies of those simple and austere colonials for the purpose of dealing with the affairs of government, were held in the same building that served as a place of worship. Such was the intimate relation between their faith and their social and political ideas.

"Latin America is the reverse of the coin. Among us Roman Catholicism has always been incompatible with democracy. During the period of the conquest and in colonial times the official religion served the purpose of weakening consciences so that the peoples would more easily tolerate despotism and be more ductile under oppression. Clerical and absolutist Spain employed the physical force of her soldiers and the moral influence of her priests in a perfect partnership which led to the enchaining of these embryonic settlements and their more easy exploitation. Democracy appeared in our lands in answer to the instinctive cry of popular agony and under the inspiration of Anglo-Saxon democracy and the emotional impulse of the French revolution. In the north democracy was born under the shadow of religion; here, among us, it appeared in spite of religion." [48]

The religion which nurtured democracy in the north was a way of life. It grew out of the very spiritual conceptions of religion

[48] " The Danger of Intolerance," by Mario Clerena Rodríguez, in *America*, May, 1943. Havana, Cuba.

which was shared by the mystics of the fourteenth century, Tau-
ler, Suso, and À Kempis. Unfortunately, during that same period
there grew up in Spain a very different conception of religion.
The eight centuries during which the Spanish people had been
fighting the Moors gradually formed in their minds the idea that
religion is loyalty to a warrior leader, to a flag, to a group, to an organization. During those eight hundred years they fought against
those who were not only enemies of the State but also of Christianity. And so the Christian became a warrior, and every warrior
seemed to become *ipso facto* a Christian. War and religion were
almost one and the same thing. Christian duty consisted in fighting. Bravery covered all sins. " The very activities of the Jesuit
order," says Luis Alberto Sánchez, " so frequently combated in
colonial South America as well as in the later republican period,
may be better understood if one remembers that the founder of
that religious order had two well defined qualities: he was a soldier and he was a Spaniard." This pugnacious and intolerant quality of the Spanish Church is still potent today in the Roman Catholicism of Latin America.

The soldiers and captains who had driven the Moors out of
Spain now turned their attention to the millions of infidels to be
dominated, plundered, and converted to Christianity. The new
world offered thrilling adventures, boundless wealth. The Spaniards lost their mental balance and rapine, lust, and cruelty characterized their invasion of the new world. " They were in their
own eyes a chosen people," says Hume, " who under the shadow
of the cross could do no evil; the Inquisition had sanctified cruelty
in the service of Christ. Confiscation and death had been the portion of their own neighbors whose orthodoxy was doubtful; plunder and expulsion had been inflicted in the name of the faith on
their Moorish kinsmen before the heaven-gazing eyes of their
saintly queen. . . . If it was welcome in the sight of God to burn
and plunder Spaniards whose doctrine was questionable, how
much more grateful would be the blood of infidel savages who had
no belief at all?" [49] It was a forcible and ruthless process. But the

[49] Hume, Martin A. S., *The Spanish People*. William Heinemann, London,
1901.

conquistadors were sincere, in spite of the mistaken methods they used and the superstitious and idolatrous nature of the faith they professed. They had not been nurtured in a religion that issued in ethical living and moral character. The sword and the cross were supposed to advance together, but usually the cross lagged far behind. Latin America had a bad start.

Dr. Enrique Molina, rector of the University of Concepción, Chile, has recently published a comparative study of the cultural-historic development of the Anglo- and Hispanic-American peoples.[50] He is interested in discovering the reasons for the superior development of the United States of North America as compared with what has been called the " disunited " states of South America. He notes the difference in genesis and development of the North and South American states. The English colonists left their home with the firm purpose of holding on to the religion which they professed. In their new home their religious faith assisted them in preserving the vigorous vital unity in which they had been schooled and which had fitted them so admirably for the conquest of a generous land.

This eminent South American educator then points out that the South Americans have had to shoulder a heritage not at all fortunate or happy. He notes their scorn of manual labor, the lack of private initiative, the disproportion between the little that they produce and the much that they consume. " As consumers," says Dr. Molina, " we are highly civilized; as producers, we are still primitives." He says that the Hispanic-American peoples are not even drawn together by the living link of a vital religion. And he concludes: " The religiousness of Catholics in Hispanic America did not generally have that medullar and dynamic center which we discovered in the people of North America, and it frequently issued in a deliquescent indifference which nothing with vital morality has been able to replace."

Ask the average thoughtful Latin American, " What is Hispanic America's most serious problem? " The answer will be: " *El problema espiritual* " (the spiritual problem), or as Dr. Alfredo Pala-

[50] *Llamado de Superacion a la América Hispana.* Published in Chile by Enrique Molina, 1943.

cios expressed it: "We need in our America the leavening of
Christian morality."

Dr. Palacios is a member of the Argentine Senate, and at the
time of our interview he had just resigned from the presidency of
the La Plata University, with its twelve thousand students. He was
ordered by the Argentine Military Government to dismiss all the
professors who had signed a national petition asking that their
constitutional rights and freedom be restored to the Argentine people. Dr. Palacios refused and handed in his resignation. He is the
idol of university students, not only in Argentina, but all over the
southern continent. On the day previous to my interview, rumor
had it that he had been arrested. I called him at his home and was
relieved to hear him say, "I am still here and expecting you tomorrow at four."

Strongly anti-imperialistic, no severer critic of American and
British big business interests is to be found in Latin America than
Alfredo Palacios. He is a powerful public speaker and few men in
that southland can sway an audience as completely as he does. I
heard him address a huge crowd of people in Buenos Aires, half
of whom stood, while for two hours he spoke on the "Problems
of America." The main problem, according to his thesis, was the
United States! But he is just as passionately committed to democracy.

He was reported to have held the opinion that missionaries were
the advance agents of foreign imperialism. You will understand
why I looked forward eagerly to my interview with him.

The large living-room study into which I was ushered was almost as interesting as the large-mustached, picturesque man whom
I was to interview. Dueling foils and pistols hung upon the walls.
Framed documents certified to his membership in cultural organizations in Colombia and Bolivia. There was a testimonial from
some Chinese colony. Diplomas indicated that he was an honorary member of the staffs of the Universities of Rio de Janeiro and
Mexico. To his right on a desk covered with books in incredible
disorder was a heavy, old-fashioned, gold watch; to his left a
loaded revolver.

I congratulated him for the splendid message which he had delivered a few days previously to the students of his university. "The leaders of our Argentine independence," he said in that message, "prepared our country to resist every ideology which aimed at mutilating the high dignity of humanity, the concept of the individual's autonomy, the inestimable value of the human personality, and the spirit of solidarity which Christianity affirmed forever."

"I am a Christian," he said to me; "but not according to the rites of the Roman Church. I feel that I am closer to Christianity than most Catholics I know."

"Are missionaries from the United States a disturbing element in Argentina?" I asked him.

"Ridiculous!" he exclaimed. "On the other hand," he continued, "we need to be disturbed on this continent. Catholicism among us has lost its spirituality. It has become very materialistic. We need in our America the leavening of Christian morality."

Latin Americans see in Protestantism many of the elements which they desire for their own religious life. Dr. Ferraz, the influential Brazilian jurist and president of the Court of Appeals, whom we have already quoted, points this out:

"Protestantism is a democratic-federative movement. The Christian Protestant world is a vast federation of churches, governed democratically in conformity with the model laid down by the primitive church. The life of the local congregations is intense and greatly contributes to the incorporation of evangelical ideals into the life of the community. It tends to the creation of a people who themselves become priests and kings. The people themselves exercise the ministry of the altar. Roman Catholicism, in its organization, follows the model of an absolute monarchy with accentuated political activities. And be it remembered: in the field of politics men will always be divided. The doctrine of Christ, on the other hand, is a power which makes for solidarity."

Thoughtful Latin Americans do not hesitate to recognize that their people are in desperate need of a religious faith which is more than formal and which issues in strength of moral character. The "acids of modernity" have led them to react bitterly against a religion of superstition.

Dr. Plinio Barreto is one of the foremost lawyers in São Paulo, Brazil. At the time of Mr. Herbert Hoover's visit to Brazil he was editor of a newspaper with the largest circulation in the state of São Paulo. A deep impression was made on Brazilians when Mr. Hoover, as Theodore Roosevelt and Mr. Bryan had done before him, refused to allow official engagements to keep him from going to church on Sunday morning. Plinio Barreto commented on this in an editorial which recognized the connection between a real religious experience and sterling moral character. We quote a few sentences:

"Nothing revealed Mr. Hoover so well . . . as the care with which on Sunday he went to attend a religious service. . . . This act reveals a man habituated to the worship of things spiritual, and one who has the courage of his faith. . . . The religious sentiment, when pure and true, is the strongest indication of high morality. The hypocrite, the fanatic, the man of superstitious practices is simply another variety of fraud. He is as impervious to moral influence as to the true light of religion.

"The superstitious man's religion, like that of the hypocrite, is not religion. It is a form of immorality. It does not elevate, it degrades. It does not inspire confidence, it puts one on his guard; it does not reveal nobility of soul, it betrays either villainy or stupidity. It is a mask, not an armor; it is a trap, not a fortress. Hoover's religion, because it is simple, because it is real, is the only kind that is fruitful and respectable."

Latin America deserves a "new deal" religiously. Vast numbers of Indians as well as others have never had a chance of knowing Christ as a personal Saviour and a transforming power. The form of Christianity which has predominated on that continent has not been able to interpret to the masses the living Christ of the Gospels or develop a high type of ethical life except in a choice minority. Democracy will with difficulty flourish in the atmosphere of religious autocracy. Personal religion and a spiritual experience that has been worked out "with fear and trembling," are the necessary bases for success in political and economic democracy. Without the ethical and deepening influence of real Christianity the South American nations will present the tragic spectacle of peoples who have won the material world but lost their souls. South America without the influence of a living Christ will be the future powder magazine of the world. It will have the brilliance of modern paganism without the inner control of religious convictions. With its man power undepleted by the present war and its immense wealth of natural resources barely scratched, it stands before its northern American neighbor as a potential friend and collaborator, if a common spiritual experience can bind the two continents, or as a possible enemy, if the irresponsible forces of selfishness and exploitation dominate the life of these young giants who are just now taking their place in the commonwealth of nations.

IX: Latin Americans Want Liberty

"BY ITS FRUIT THE TREE IS KNOWN. IF PROTESTANTISM HAS GIVEN US nations like the very liberal American Republic of the North where Catholicism is in a minority, why not accept its beneficial influence in the working out of Brazil's destiny?" So said the distinguished Brazilian, Dr. Raimundo Nogueira de Faria, in his statement to me. This writer, journalist, member of the law faculty of the University of Pará, and member of the Appellate Court of the State of Pará, then continues:

"It would not be possible to deny this truth which history teaches: Progress stagnates in countries where the formation of the popular spirit is kept under priestly control. Italy is famous for its devotion to the arts, Portugal for the audacity of its famous navigators, and Spain owes the glory of its golden period to the fearless and leonine daring of its *Conquistadores*. But it is undeniable that when you think of the greatness of Holland and England, for instance, you recall not so much similar qualities of heroism, but rather the staunch religious virtues which Protestantism bred in their people."

The architect-engineer who is erecting the highest building in Mexico City said that a Christian revolution was needed in Latin America, a revolution that would be the result of the application of Christian principles to the solution of all our problems. Catholicism and Protestantism ought to be united against the common enemy, he thought.

"Should American Roman Catholics send missionaries of their faith to Mexico?" I asked him.

"Well, that might help a little," he answered. "Much would depend on what kind of missionaries they send. I would prefer one Protestant missionary who comes with a Christian spirit and compels us to think, to ten Catholic missionaries who would do nothing to stir up our minds!"

"It is said that Protestant work is negative, that it deprives the

114

Catholic of his faith and then abandons him to his unbelief. Is this true?" I asked Dr. Nuñez Regueiro, the distinguished Uruguayan intellectual whom I have already quoted.

"This affirmation is most absurd," he answered. "From my own personal observation, I would say that practically all the people converted in our time to Protestantism were originally Catholic. For the most part their parents were Catholics, or indifferent to religion. The Catholic turns Protestant, precisely because he finds among the Evangelicals a new faith which he did not have before, a faith which has something and means something, which knows what it wants and where it is going. The faith of the Catholic, if it was faith in Christ, deepens when he becomes a Protestant. And this faith feeds on new bread, unknown before, which comes from a direct knowledge of the wisdom of the Bible, the book very sacred to the Protestant. My father, son of a Spanish doctor, and member of a family of Catholic priests and bishops, was an acolyte in Spain, and studied Latin with the parish priest. But he abandoned the religion of his fathers and became an atheist. Then he was converted to the Gospel in a Methodist Church. From then on he devoted himself to making his life more holy. I trust that I shall never forget the inspiration and enrichment which I gained from hearing him read the New Testament when I was a small boy, and from the lessons which I studied in a Methodist Sunday School. And I desire with all my heart that this shall be the best legacy which I leave my sons, whom I am instructing in these same teachings. My personal testimony is, therefore, that Protestants as well as many Catholics who have been converted to the Gospel, have not only not lost their faith, but they have seen it vivified and deepened by a clearer and more intimate knowledge of the law and love of Christ. No one that I know of, who has really been influenced by Protestantism, has fallen into the night of unbelief. All of them confess that once they were 'blind,' but now they 'see,' in the Gospel sense. I openly proclaim this truth and give God the praise. And it is the best answer to the question regarding the value of Protestant work in the region of the River Plate."

In the United States where the clergy is usually held in high esteem and where organized religion has not been a dead weight on progress, it is hard to understand Latin America's bitter and often unreconcilable hostility to the clergy. I was interviewing one of Argentina's leading lawyers, Dr. Enrique Jorge, a man of brilliant career whose charming spirit revealed all the fine points of a deep Spanish culture. He is a prominent member of the Bar Association; former editor of the Argentine law journal *Revista Jurídica y Ciencias Sociales;* corresponding member of " The Institute of Brazilian Lawyers," and the author of five or six books on legal problems. As we talked of the " fiercely " liberal and anticlerical spirit which has been present all through the history of Latin America, he told me the story of his father's last illness.

" He called me to his bedside," said Dr. Jorge, " and said, ' They will probably call in a priest when I am dying and that will provide me with some pleasant entertainment, for I shall have some little questions to put to him '! "

The morning he was to be operated upon, sensing the seriousness of his condition, he called his son, and in the presence of his sister and sister-in-law, both devout Roman Catholics, he said: " In my last moments do not bring a priest to my bedside *even though I may ask for him.*" He feared that in extreme physical weakness his mind might not be clear enough to hold firmly to his lifelong convictions.

" I am a Christian," said Dr. Jorge to me, " though I am not a member of any Church. I believe in the Church, in what is Divine in the Church, in what is really spiritual. I like to make a distinction between religion and the Church. They are not always equivalent. I do not believe in the Church as a political organization."

" Should we Protestants voluntarily withdraw from a country if we are unpopular and not wanted? " I asked him.

" Not at all," he answered with great emphasis; " you should go where you are needed and not only where you are wanted. Jesus was not wanted in many places; they stoned him at times; but He went on with his mission. There is a great field for Protestant work in this country. There are many Roman Catholics who are deeply dissatisfied with the spiritual condition of the Church. Many others are anticlerical. The Latin peoples have a profound spiritual sensibility. They dislike being adrift spiritually and culturally, so the tendency is strong in them to preserve an outward or nominal relation to the Church, though they may long ago have hopelessly given up all belief in her dogmas. Religion has become to them a social function, one of the amenities of life."

As Luis Alberto Sánchez points out, the history of Latin America is the story of the struggle of submerged groups against exploitation and enslavement. The history of the period of independence develops, he says, "under the inspiration of the cult of free thought. All the political founders of our independence were free thinkers as were also the majority of the intellectual leaders of that period." The future of Latin America lies, not with the conservative-reactionary groups of Latin America but with the legitimate successors of these early believers in freedom.

What Latin Americans cannot understand is why the United States has so frequently favored the semitotalitarian dictatorships when it intervened in the affairs of Latin America, and when it had the opportunity of following the principles that inspired the democratic founders of this great American commonwealth, it sought refuge behind the principle of nonintervention — a principle, however, which was not applied against the dictatorships.[51] Is it unreasonable for our southern neighbors to expect the foreign policy of the United States to reflect the domestic principles of freedom which have contributed so much to this country's greatness?

There is no uncertainty as to what the collective Latin-American will is as regards the Four Freedoms. The common people of Latin America take their stand unhesitatingly by the side of the nations fighting today for freedom.

Can you blame them for wondering why the United States, which now fights for freedom and democracy in the "tyrants' war," took part, nevertheless, in the destruction of the Spanish republic? Can you blame them for thinking that people who acclaim Franco as a Christian hero have a strange conception of Christianity, that the Vatican's backing of Franco has hopelessly compromised the Roman Catholic Church which they feel has

[51] An identical complaint is made by Luis Alberto Sánchez in his recent book *Un Sudamericano en Norteamerica*, p. 67. Ercilla, Santiago, Chile, 1943.

toyed too much with Fascism and dictatorship and is opposed to real freedom and radical reform?

Noticias Gráficas, one of the leading evening papers of Buenos Aires, in August of 1943, attributed Argentina's failure to break off relations with the Axis powers to "certain civilian groups of ultramontane ideology who are trying to push us into a trap of some kind of dictatorship." The editorial placed responsibility for Argentina's unfortunate position squarely upon "the Axis sympathizers, disguised today with the euphemistic title of a Catholicism which they neither feel nor practice, the same Catholicism which in Spain handed over that country to the violence of Nazi barbarism."

When General Fulgencia Batista, who was then president of Cuba, visited the United States in January, 1943, the reporters asked him what would be the effect in South America if the Allies should invade Spain. General Batista answered that such a move would meet with total support in all Latin-American countries. He was not speaking for the hierarchy of the Roman Catholic Church, but he was representing the sentiments of the overwhelming majority of the people in the southern nations, people whose sympathy and good will go out to the Protestant Church because they have seen that wherever Protestantism has gone freedom has become a reality.

Latin Americans want freedom and democracy. A most encouraging sign of new life within Roman Catholicism in Latin America is the appearance of small but vigorous groups of thinkers who see that the political alliance of their Church with the conservative-reactionary political parties is having disastrous consequences. *Orden Cristiano*, a Roman Catholic weekly published in Buenos Aires, in its issue of April 15, 1943, strongly condemns the tendency of Roman Catholicism to ally itself with the conservative right-wing political parties. It advocates what it calls "liberalism with God." It says, "The prudent Catholic should not allow himself to be classed with the right-wing tendency in politics which so often supports ideals of doubtful morality." It quotes *Tribuna Católica*, the organ of the Catholic Action in Uruguay, as condemning "the tendency of identifying conservatism with Catholicism, and liberalism with anti-Catholicism. Solidarity with the right-wing groups has been costly to Catholicism. These groups have sheltered under the standard of religion political purposes and ideals that the social doctrines of the Church and the Christian defense of the rights of the oppressed, cannot help but condemn." It then goes on, with singular courage, to say that the time has come to favor a Christian left-wing tendency in Catholicism.

Another example of the struggle for a more democratic orientation within Roman Catholicism in Latin America is the public discussion going on in Chile at this writing, between the Young Catholics of the Falange Nacional (no relation to the Spanish Fascist Falange) and Father Luis Arturo Pérez, a Roman Catholic priest. One point in the discussion involves Professor Jacques Maritain's demand for equal rights for all religions. Father Pérez contends that " Maritain's position means absolute liberty of conscience, a doctrine condemned by Pope Pius IX in the Syllabus of Errors and by Pope Leo XIII in the encyclical *Libertas e Immortale*." Therefore, argues Pérez, Maritain's philosophy is absurd, "because he is promoting ideas which have already been condemned by the popes, whose doctrines philosophers as well as non-philosophers must respect and obey." The Young Catholics reply: " If the most Christian and realistic declarations of Maritain are in opposition to the teachings of the popes, we dare to follow what our consciences consider the more Christian attitude."

Latin Americans claim freedom to dissent from a State- or Church-imposed uniformity. Every great movement begins with individuals or small groups that break away from their environment, protest against corruption, and live as strangers and sojourners in this world. It is important, therefore, to be able to distinguish between a heretic who would undermine a faith and the one who seeks to purify it of its corruptions. These dissenters, who so frequently initiated a stream of new life that rejuvenated society, were determined to obey God rather than man. Christ himself is the supreme nonconformist or Protestant of history. He stood out against much that was traditional in the religion of his day.

Latin Americans, therefore, claim the right to heresy! " Where the right to heresy is not recognized," says Alberto Rembao, Mexican editor of *La Nueva Democracia*,[52] " there is no democracy. Without heresy there is no progress, for all the great movements of the human spirit had heretical beginnings and were considered heterodox by the established systems which they overturned. True democracy conceives the possibility of itself being improved upon. . . . The right to heresy is the right to launch out toward the frontiers of knowledge. The heretic is one who ventures out, who asks for freedom to dissent, who claims the prerogative of abandoning ancient and accepted land marks in his search for new realms. . . . Democracy is rational and recognizes the fallibility of its agencies. A majority should never tolerate; it should respect. A wise society will know that these ferments of rebellion will die a natural death unless they carry in them some true seed of real life."

[52] *La Nueva Democracia*, June, 1944. Committee on Cooperation in Latin America, 156 Fifth Avenue, New York City.

X: Status of Protestant Missions in Latin America

THE PROTESTANT MOVEMENT IN LATIN AMERICA — WHICH HAS PRO-
duced a Moises Sáenz, who at the time of his death in 1942 was
Mexican ambassador to Peru; a Professor Monteverde, of the National University of Uruguay; a Justo Cubiló, member of the Supreme Court of Uruguay; an Erasmo Braga, of Brazil — deserves
something more than a journalistic report, which is all that I can
give it in this brief chapter.

As early as 1557 a small party of Huguenots landed in Brazil
and established a branch of the Reformed Church of Geneva.
Later on some foreign communities of Reformed faith living under the colonial rules, such as the Dutch, the British, and the
German, attempted to organize themselves as Churches in Brazil
and other areas, but freedom of worship was consistently refused
them.

Between 1804 and 1807 the British and Foreign Bible Society
published twenty thousand copies of the New Testament in Portu-
guese. These were distributed along the Brazilian coast by mer-
chants and seafaring men interested in the distribution of the
Scriptures.

The first Protestant body to obtain a foothold in South America
was the Anglican. A congregation in Brazil was organized for
members of the Anglican communion. The new Church was begun in 1819, and became the first non-Roman Catholic place of
worship to be built in South America.[53]

In 1818, James Thomson, of the British and Foreign Bible
Society, landed in Buenos Aires shortly after Argentina had secured its independence. Thomson introduced the Lancasterian
school system, and his educational projects received the warmest
support from the leaders of the fight for independence in all the
countries that he visited. In Buenos Aires a hundred schools were

[53] See Mackay, John A., *The Other Spanish Christ*, pp. 231 *et al.* Macmillan, 1933.

organized. The textbook used for instruction in reading was the Bible. Thomson was made an honorary citizen of Argentina, and later of Chile. In Peru, where he arrived in 1822, the liberator San Martín turned the friars out of a monastery in order that Thomson might set up his school.

In the year 1867 in the city of Buenos Aires another Thomson, Dr. John Francis Thomson, preached the first Protestant Spanish sermon delivered in South America. At about that same time President Sarmiento, of Argentina, asked an American missionary, Dr. Goodfellow, to contract a number of normal-school teachers in North America. Sixty-three teachers arrived, and in 1871 the first normal school in Argentina was founded.

Many English and Scottish soldiers and officers formed part of the armies that fought for independence in South America. In Bolivar's army there was a British Legion. Many of the officers settled in the South American countries. One of these, Colonel Fraser, settled in Colombia and later became secretary of war. He married a Colombian lady. He and an influential group of patriots saw that the South American countries would never really be free until Christianity became a vital spiritual force among them. In 1850 they sent to Scotland for a clergyman. But there were no funds then for the sending of missionaries from Scotland. The American Presbyterian Board, however, responded to the call, and in 1856 Horace Pratt went to Colombia. Thus it was that Protestant work was begun at the invitation of people in Colombia.

A Scottish sheep farmer in Peru was taken to task by neighboring Peruvian farmers for his scrupulous and fair dealings with the Indians. He explained that his religious convictions would not allow him to take advantage of their ignorance. Some days later the neighbors came to him saying that they wanted him to bring a teacher out from England to inculcate in their sons a religion that produced such sterling character. This resulted in the bringing of the first Protestant missionary to Peru.

Today the total Protestant community in Latin America is reckoned at about 2,000,000. Protestant membership records do not tell the full story of Protestant influence. In the state of Rio

Grande, Brazil, for instance, Methodist official records report a membership of 5,000; but in the national census 25,000 declared they were Methodists!

There are 52 theological colleges and Bible institutes in Latin America; 60 hospitals and clinics, and this widespread Protestant community reads 155 Church papers and periodicals. One of the finest printing presses in Buenos Aires is the Methodist Imprenta. The Union Publishing House, in Buenos Aires, La Aurora, published 49 books during 1943. This is only one of 10 Protestant bookstores and publishing houses in that important city and suburbs. There are 12 publishing houses and booksellers in Brazil.

Mission farms can be found all over Latin America: 5 of them in Brazil; " El Vergel," in Chile, with its nearly 4,000 acres, its 4 missionary farm experts, and nearly 1,000 people, men, women, and children, living on the land and learning the latest and best methods of farming; up in the highlands of Bolivia and Peru, among the Indians, the splendid Seventh Day Adventist Missions; and on Lake Titicaca, the Canadian Baptist Farm Mission.

Illiteracy in South America ranges from 80 per cent in the northern republics to 40 per cent in the southern countries. It is difficult for democracy to succeed in countries where masses of the population are submerged in ignorance. Protestantism is a religion with a book. Wherever it goes it takes the Bible. It is a faith that cannot be professed by illiterates, as the great Argentine president, Sarmiento, once pointed out. Consequently Protestantism establishes schools and colleges. Its schools cover the southern continent and today, as during the past seventy-five years, they are turning out thousands of well-trained young men and women. It was the Protestant Church that inaugurated the present continent-wide campaign against illiteracy which is being enthusiastically supported by the South American Governments.

There are 152 secondary schools, besides many elementary schools.

Among the outstanding educational institutions of missionary origin, or which continue to function under missionary auspices, are the following: Mackenzie College, in São Paulo, Brazil (some of the finest engineers in that country are graduates of the engineering department of this college); Bennett College for girls, in Rio de Janeiro, with an attendance of 579; Ward College, with a total enrollment that now reaches 1,000; Crandon Institute, Montevideo, with 590 enrollment; Santiago College, Santiago, Chile, with 650 enrollment; Instituto Inglés, Santiago, with over 400 enrollment; Colegio Internacional, in Asunción, the best school in Paraguay; Gammon Institute, Lavras, and Granberry, in Juiz de Fora, both in Brazil. In Cuba there is Colegio Internacional of the Baptists, La Progresiva of the Presbyterians, and Candler College of the Methodists; in Puerto Rico the Polytechnic Institute, surpassed only by the University of Puerto Rico.

A number of these schools have pioneered along lines that were new to our southern neighbors. Crandon Institute, Montevideo, established the first course in home economics offered in South America. Bennett College, Rio de Janeiro, has the first prekindergarten department in the southern continent. Most of the Protestant schools are coeducational. Latin Americans who looked askance at coeducation are beginning to see that, far from bringing the scandalous results they feared, it works and has decided advantages. In Barranquilla, Colombia, encouraged by the example of the two large Presbyterian schools in that city, the Government held joint commencement exercises for their boys' and girls' schools, an epoch-making departure.

I asked the well-known Argentine lawyer and educator, Dr. Jorge: " Do Protestant schools proselytize? "

" They do not," was his answer. " A large proportion of their students are from Catholic families and some of their teachers also belong to that faith. An illustration of the tolerance and real ' catholicity ' of the Protestants which we admire is the case of the Methodist girls' school in Rosario. There are three Roman Catholic teachers in that school. When it was asked why they were not replaced by Protestant teachers, the answer was: they have fulfilled their mission faithfully and well; it would not be just to dismiss them. American mission schools as well as American Protestant missionaries are doing much to interpret the real United States to Argentina."

Protestants have taken the Bible to Latin America. Portions of the Scriptures have been translated into many of the Indian dialects. In some cases these dialects first had to be reduced to written form. Millions of copies of the Scriptures have been circulated by the largest of the Bible societies, the British and Foreign Bible Society and the American Bible Society.

Social service centers abound. La Boca Mission, in one of the most congested sections of Buenos Aires, offers free kindergarten, a gymnasium, a boys' club, classes in arts and crafts for men and women, a free medical clinic, and sports facilities. In Puerto Rico is the Marina Neighborhood House, with its kindergarten and primary school, a day nursery and milk distribution center. In Chile there is the Sweet Memorial and the Maternity Center *Madre e Hijo;* in Montevideo, Uruguay, the Cerro Mission and Goodwill Industries. These are only a few examples of Christlike service which is being rendered to communities that are afflicted with grave social evils.

There are some great Protestant Churches and congregations in Latin America. In São Paulo there is the Igreja Unida, with 1,200 members and 1,500 in the Sunday School. Forty laymen of that Church have charge of 11 preaching places distributed throughout the city. There is the Gante Methodist Church, in Mexico City, as well as the Presbyterian Church of the Divino Salvador. The Mandamientos Church in Lima, Peru, gathers a large and enthusiastic congregation, not only on Sunday, but during the week. The two large Pentecostal congregations in Santiago, Chile, rarely have fewer than 1,000 persons present at their average services. Central Church, Montevideo, has a cathedral-like building that honors that beautiful city. Much of the Protestant work in Latin America is self-supporting and self-governing. One of the largest denominations at work in Uruguay and Argentina reports that its work is 97 per cent self-supporting.

These and thousands of other congregations are singing their Gospel to the people around them. There is no singing in the Rotary Clubs of South America because the Latins have not been trained in community or congregational singing. Protestantism is singing its way into the hearts of Latin Americans.

" The greatest hope of the Protestant Church in Latin America today is found in the young people. . . ."[54] In February, 1941, the first Congress of Evangelical Youth in Latin America was held in Lima, Peru. Fifty delegates representing 20 denominations and 12 countries met in spite of enormous difficulties. One of the results of this conference was the formation of a continent-wide federation of Latin-American Protestant youth.

There is an increasing movement toward a closer co-operation in Spanish America between the different Protestant groups. In Guatemala several denominations have joined to form a synod which looks forward to an indigenous Church. Most of the Protestant work in the Dominican Republic is under the direction of a unique missionary organization, the Board for Christian Work in Santo Domingo, in which three denominations, the Presbyterian, Methodist, and United Brethren, pool their resources.[55]

A few years ago I had to stop off at the pumping station and filters of the Montevideo water system, miles away on the Santa Lucía River. From there I was to go to the little town of Santa Lucía for a service in our Protestant chapel. It was ordinarily a roundabout route, first by coach, then by rail. "I'll provide you with horses," said the engineer in charge of this important plant, "and you can cut across country, through the woods, to your destination."

"But I do not know the way," I said.

"I'll give you a guide."

When I caught sight of my guide standing by our horses, I stopped. He was a dangerous-looking individual, almost pure Indian, dark-skinned and with longish hair. The scar of a deep cut disfigured his face. When my friend saw my hesitation, he laughed.

"I'll tell you something about this man. He was the most dangerous *cuatrero* (cattle thief) in all this territory. At one time the government sent out a company of soldiers to try and catch him, but they didn't succeed."

"Well, brother," I said to him, "and what have I done to you that you should entrust me to such a man?"

---

[54] See Rycroft, W. Stanley, *On This Foundation*, pp. 86, 87. Friendship Press, 1942.

[55] *Ibid.*, p. 79.

" Don't worry," was his answer, " he is the best foreman we have on the works and he is also a deacon in the little church where you are to be tonight."

That was interesting! Former cattle thief and now the best foreman and a Church deacon. How did it happen? Thereby hangs another tale — the story of how a Danish ex-sailor, who roamed the country with horse and buggy and Bibles, one day entered the old Gaucho's mud hut on the banks of the Santa Lucía and read to him and to his woman a chapter of the Bible and then knelt for prayer. The Gaucho wanted to brain the gringo, but something very kindly in George Petersen's face held back the cruel hand. Other visits followed, and one day when Petersen knelt the woman knelt too. And finally came the great day when the cattle thief knelt on the adobe floor and something began to work in his life.

There he was, that evening, with his wife in one of the front pews. Don Juan Daré — he had a name now! Next day I went around for maté: I wanted to see the ex-cattle-thief in his home. I wonder if the engineer in charge of the Montevideo water system " resents " the presence of Protestant pastors and missionaries? I'd like to ask him also if there are not still many more " heathen " left in South America, as there are in Chicago and New York, who might be touched by the Old Book and a Christian prayer and moved by the good face of a gentle man!

XI: Protestant Missions in Latin America Must Continue

IN THE COURSE OF MY RECENT JOURNEY OVER LATIN AMERICA I CON-
sidered it important to get in touch with representatives of the
Department of State and of the co-ordinator's office. A conversation which I sustained with one of the cultural attachés is of
especial interest.

When I was ushered into his office I opened the conversation by
telling him of my interest in the Catholic-Protestant controversy
over Latin America.

"It is a very serious problem," he said. "I don't know what is
going to happen with the coming of fanatical and extremist Protestant groups."

"But how can you keep them out?" I asked. "Isn't this one of
the inevitable drawbacks of democracy? To suppress or repress
these dissident groups would lead us into Fascism or totalitarianism."

"They are a discredit to the United States!" he insisted.

"But have there not been many business representatives who
have also been a discredit to the United States?" I asked. "Would
you therefore advocate keeping all American businessmen out of
Latin America?"

"I don't see that there is much strength to that argument," he
countered. "If unworthy businessmen come to these countries,
that is no reason why we should countenance the entrance of these
religious troublemakers. I recognize the splendid work the Presbyterian schools are doing in this country. Who could deny that
the increase in such educational establishments would mean much
for the awakening and progress of this country?"

"But," I said, "the Catholics do not make that distinction between wise and unwise Protestants. Here, as well as in the United
States, they are constantly saying that these schools exist solely
for the purpose of proselyting."

"You can see the difficult position in which the Government in Washington finds itself," he said. "There it is under pressure from the Protestants. Here it is under pressure from the Catholics."

I had to deny the first part of his statement. "There is no organized Protestant pressure being exerted in Washington and the State Department knows it," I said. "But there is a very definite and persistent campaign carried on in the United States by the Roman Catholic hierarchy to discredit Protestant work in South America, and great influence has been brought to bear on the State Department to get it to refuse passports to outgoing Protestant missionaries. Individual mission board secretaries have tried to find out why they were being discriminated against while Catholic missionaries and visiting priests and nuns were given every facility for getting to South America. You wouldn't call that exerting pressure, would you? Personally, I am glad that these fine American priests and sisters have come to South America. They are morally and intellectually superior to most of their colleagues on this continent."

"There precisely," he said, "is the problem. Would you compare the training and intellectual condition of these Catholics with the mentality of the Jehovah's Witnesses?"

"But," I objected, "is it fair of you to compare some of the poorest among Protestants with the best among Catholics?"

Somewhere in the conversation my interlocutor interjected this unconscious tribute to the value of Protestant missions: "I know Spanish Catholicism. It is at one pole, and American Catholicism is at the other. The Spanish Church has had no competition and it has gone to seed. I am not forgetting the value of competition even in the realm of religion."

"One result of interviews and conversations with Latin-American leaders of thought," I told him, "is that of making me feel very confident that the problem of the relations between Catholics and Protestants in Latin America will gradually adjust itself if the members of the Catholic hierarchy in the United States will keep their hands off. Protestants will know how to get on with their Catholic neighbors in the southern lands if the problem of achieving religious liberty is not aggravated by influences emanating from the United States." Further, I reminded the attaché that Protestants already have been living in Latin America for a little over a hundred years. "Protestant missions are not new on this continent," I continued. "They have a long and honorable record back of them. If the Catholics in the United States will cease trying to convert a religious problem into one that is political, we shall come out better Catholics and better Protestants in South America as a result of our spiritual rivalry."

"I think that it would be best to silence the whole matter . . . ," said my friend.

"Well, who started the trouble?" was my answer. "It was the American hierarchy, strong in its feelings of political power in Washington, that started the campaign by means of magazine articles, radio talks, episcopal proclamations, and other aggressive methods. Many of their statements have been either false or were only half-truths. They have carried on a campaign that was manifestly unfair."

"Would it not be best to say nothing? to turn the other cheek?"

"That's what we have been doing in the hope that their aggressiveness would diminish. But in the interest of fair play and for the sake of sound and intelligent relations between the two Americas, the time has come to speak up."

As I rose to leave I said: "Doctor, I dislike these fanatical Protestants as much as you do, and they don't like me! But just when I am tempted to side in with those who would like to keep them out of South America, I remember some of the homes these people have established in the cities and villages of Latin America; lovely American homes they are. Not lovely because of furniture or equipment. Not many of them have electric refrigerators or innerspring mattresses. But lovely because they enshrine the American ideal of home life. For these Protestant missionaries go out, the married men each with a wife and usually with children, and in such homes the American respect for womanhood is seen; the Christian nurture of little children is demonstrated; the care of the home, the preparation of food, the abstention from the use of narcotics, are all positive and helpful contributions to Latin-American life. As one remembers all this, it becomes apparent that the by-products of the activities of even the tightly creed-bound religionists may sometimes be among the most creative contributions made by Protestant missions."

So much for the interview with the attaché.

There is an element of high adventure in any effort to convey a particular philosophy or gospel to others. It is not a safe and sane calling! One can't predict what the outcome will be.

"Those who try to bring mankind to their own specific way of seeing God will always incur the reproach of the broad for their narrowness, the ridicule of the worldly wise for their lack of humor, and the angry rebuke of disturbed statesmen to whom they are at best intrusive busybodies." So says Professor William E. Hocking, of Harvard.[56] Then he concludes: "Yet the work they have done bears the nearest trait of disinterested good will that the world affords; and its fruits, direct and incidental, have left marks on history of which mankind will ever think with reverence as well as gratitude, and which would have been possible to no other conceivable motive."

Protestantism will make no apologies for its interest in missions, nor will it be impressed by arguments which are used in favor of a moratorium on such activities during this war period. "The Christian faith has begun some of its most significant advances in the midst of what to contemporaries appeared disastrous and overwhelming reverses," says Professor Kenneth S. Latourette, ". . . in times of seeming disaster, in ways which would have eluded the casual observer . . . from Christianity have issued new movements which have led the faith to fresh achievements."[57] Professor Latourette then points out that the modern missionary movement was started in the days when the world was in great turmoil and the French Revolution was approaching the peak of its violence. "In 1795, when the wars of the French Revolution were well under way, the London Missionary Society

[56] In a pamphlet, *Evangelism.*
[57] "Missions and Wars," in *The International Review of Missions,* October, 1942.

was organized," he says. "In 1797, in spite of the fact that Holland was occupied by the French, the Netherlands Missionary Society was inaugurated."

In the troublous times of 1812, just before the second war between the United States and Great Britain, and while American ships were being held up and searched by the British, a group of missionaries dared to run the blockade and sailed for the Orient. In spite of great difficulties of transportation Robert Morrison reached China. At the time, these enterprises for spreading the Gospel may have seemed out of place in a world of war. But the perspective we have gained allows us to see that the really significant events of those stormy days were not the overshadowing victories or defeats of warring armies, but the missionary undertakings which were inaugurated and which have borne rich fruitage in Christian allies in the Orient. Generalissimo and Madame Chiang Kai-shek are among the valuable returns of that missionary effort.

What is the attitude of Protestants toward the problem which has concerned us in this book?

The Protestant position is that the realm of religious truth should be just as open and free as every other realm of knowledge and experience — that is, open to everyone. Hence the Protestant Churches have translated and published the Bible in many hundreds of languages throughout the world.

If chemistry, physics, astronomy, and biology had been hampered by some self-perpetuating body of men who insisted upon suppressing every new idea, would these sciences have developed the vast realm of knowledge we have today? Why, then, can we not trust absolute freedom of research and experiment in the study of the Bible and of religious phenomena and experience, as we do in other fields of truth? The basic principle of a sound Protestantism surely calls for just that.

In the first place, we stand for the universal priesthood of all believers. We believe that by himself and "on his own" the Christian can pray directly to the Father, and can read and study the Bible and come to his own conclusions as to its meanings, values, and challenges. Instead of confessing his sins to a priest, he can confess them directly to God. There is no end of obscurantism in Protestantism to this day. The principle of higher criticism still fights for its chance with a multitude of people. But Protestantism has taught the layman not only to pray and to read the Bible for himself — working out his own salvation, as the apostle expressed it — but also always to think for himself, to discriminate between differing authorities, and ultimately to decide religious matters for himself. So the second basic principle of Protestantism is the right or privilege of private judgment in the realm of religion as in other realms of experience and life. While Protestantism recognizes the need and value of scholarship and training and spiritual insight and character for the interpretation of the Bible, nevertheless it has never credited infallibility to its pastors, scholars, and saints. There is liberty in most Protestant Churches for each individual to think through his own religion and to arrive at conclusions for himself. It is true that this right of private judgment has resulted in a great variety of religious organizations and Churches, yet the remarkable thing is that among all the divisions of Protestantism there is a real undercurrent of spiritual unity. While there are great differences of theological creed and of Church polity, there is essentially little difference in ideals of moral character and of spiritual life.

Protestantism has championed liberty of thought in religion, in the faith that truth and progress are more likely to survive in freedom than in restraint, even though it be restraint growing out of high and holy purposes. The true Protestant will not accept religion brought to him on a platter any more than he will take his ideas on politics or science or literature in that way. That does not imply that he does not believe in religious leadership, in expert testimony, and in special training for interpreting the truths of Holy Scriptures: it means only that he refuses to accept any human authorities as infallible.

The Reformation is far more than the views of Luther or of Calvin, for these views were naturally limited by the age. Its real significance is to be found in the Renaissance quest for realism as against traditionalism and ecclesiastical authority. It was the struggle, to use a phrase of Carlyle, " of men intent on the essences of

things against men intent on the forms and semblances of things."
Its marks were a passion for "reality" and sincerity, for the deepest insights of the soul, and it involved an insistence upon intellectual and spiritual freedom.

Protestants believe that Christianity tended to retrograde when it allowed theology to get into the hands of ecclesiastical lawyers who conceived of the Church as an institution needing rulers after the manner of the State, a conception from which Latin Christianity to this day has been unable to emancipate itself.

Protestantism asks nothing of the State anywhere except such liberty and independence as it already now enjoys in most Protestant countries, and which, chiefly through Protestant influence, the Roman Catholic Church also enjoys in these same countries.

But all this places a large responsibility on Protestantism. We stand for freedom and for democracy. But are we as conscious as we ought to be of our own weaknesses and of certain quite illiberal tendencies among us?

Protestants, if we are faithful to our Gospel, may always tend to be disturbers of the peace. But this lays upon us a responsibility for knowing how to advocate or plead our case wisely and creatively. Some Protestants whose zeal is likely to exceed their wisdom need to remember Shakespeare's words:

> "Heat not a furnace for your foe so hot
> That it do singe yourself."

Then again, Protestantism's sectarian proliferation should fill us with shame. Time and time again we have seen Latin Americans turn away in deep perplexity from a grievously fragmentized Protestantism. It has been well said that this is our deep sin. In the conflict between a Protestant's loyalty to the Church and his individual convictions of theological doctrine, he has felt quite free to quit one body and to start another.

The totalitarian ambitions of the Roman Catholic Church in the United States and in Latin America in the field of ecclesiastical controls are to be resisted by all means that are appropriate. Such means must include political action by citizens who have the cause of religious freedom at heart. But all such efforts will avail little

unless Protestantism can learn better how to integrate and mobilize its own divided forces. Our divisiveness is no match for the
aggressiveness of a united Catholicism, ably guided by astute and
skillful leaders.

And what will the attitude of the Roman Catholics be to the
problem we have been examining? How do they propose to combine the gospel of the Four Freedoms (if indeed they accept that
gospel) with the doctrine of a closed continent for Roman Catholics?

It is idle to obscure the differences between us. We shall have
to learn that there is little possibility of building a world order
upon an absolutely common culture. Any organization making a
better world will test man's capacity for tolerance. We shall have
to learn to live and work with peoples who base their life ideals
and standards on presuppositions different from our own. There
must, of course, be some common denominator for the new world
order. Do not Protestant and Roman Catholic Christians have in
Christ that sure foundation on which to build?

Is it too much to hope that we may be able to win the confidence
and help of liberal American Catholics? Surely they see the dangers, both to their Church and to the cause of democracy, inherent
in the reactionary aggressiveness of that arrogant minority in their
Church that exercises pressure on officeholders, the press, the
stage, and the movies, and does not hesitate to threaten, coerce,
and boycott.

In spite of our differences there is much that we have in common. Saint Francis belongs to us both. The glorious cathedrals
built by pious men of the Middle Ages are Roman-Catholic-in-
spired, but they are ours too; we Protestants feel very much at
home in them. But we should feel even more at home in the basil-
icas that date back to the end of the Roman Empire. And the
more authentic our Protestant witness, the more we shall feel at
home in the catacombs, or in the home sanctuaries where Aquila
and Priscilla worshiped and where congregations in Philippi and
Corinth and Antioch met. But for the Protestant, the supreme
cathedral of faith is to be found in the Upper Room where the
followers of our common Lord and Master "were all together."

Pope Pius XI's encyclical on the Church in Germany declares that "the believer has an inalienable right to profess his faith and to practice it in the manner suited to him. Laws which suppress or render difficult the profession and practice of this faith are contrary to natural law." [58] This is also good, and quite a Protestant doctrine.

The present Pope in his 1941 Christmas message, referring to the catastrophe of war and the possibility of the frustration of peace efforts, says: "To avoid so great a calamity, it is necessary in the formulation of that peace to insure the co-operation, with sincerity and good will, not only of this or that party, or of this or that people, but also rather of all peoples and all humanity. It is a universal undertaking which requires the collaboration of all Christendom in connection with the religious and moral aspects of the new structure which must be built." [59]

There is a religious function to be served by the diversity which exists within this Christendom. But it is the function of variety, not of rivalry. Recognizing this truth, Christopher Dawson, the well-known English Catholic writer, says: "It is right that Italian peasants and the English shopkeepers should express their feelings in different forms; what is wrong is that they should worship different Gods or should regard each other as separated from the mind of Christ and the body of the Church because they speak a different language and respond to different emotional stimuli. In other words: difference of rite ought not to involve differences of faith." [60]

Defending the principle of diversity, Mr. Dawson further says: "If it had been possible to keep life to a dead level of uniformity, in which Englishmen and Spaniards, Frenchmen and Germans, were all alike, conditions might be more favorable to religious unity, but European civilization would have been immensely poorer and less vital, and its religious life would probably have been impoverished and devitalized as well. . . . If we condemn the principles of diversity or polarity in history, and demand an

[58] *Mit brennender Sorge,* 34 and 35.
[59] I have translated this from a Spanish version.
[60] *The Judgment of the Nations,* p. 174. Sheed and Ward, 1942.

abstract, uniform civilization which will obviate the risk of wars and religious schisms, we are offending against life in the same way as though we condemned the difference of the sexes, as many heretics actually have done, because it leads to immorality. . . . Small states like Switzerland and Belgium which do not even speak a common language may nevertheless possess a strong national character and historic traditions which cannot be denied in the interests of any racial theory or party ideology." [61]

There are further encouraging signs. Even in some of the older Roman Catholic lands voices are being raised urging a democratic and really Christian policy toward people of other faiths. In a recent statement issued by European Roman Catholics now exiled in the United States we find these noble sentiments:

"In social life, it is important to affirm, very forcefully, that which is commonly called freedom of conscience. Adherence to religion is an act of conscience that must be subject to the dictates of reason and divine enlightenment. It is not the state's business either to dominate or to control conscience. Those churches that in the present state of religious division share the adherence of the souls, must enjoy freedom to establish their rites, to preach their doctrines, to edify souls, to exercise their apostolate, without any interference from civil authorities in the field that belongs to religion. . . . It is Christianity itself that lays down the foundations of civil tolerance in religious matters. . . . We repudiate every measure of discrimination against any religious or racial group." [62]

Among the signatures are such noted names as Paul van Zeeland, Don Luigo Sturzo, J. A. de Aguirre, Jacques and Raissa Maritain, Sigrid Undset, Sir Philip Gibbs, and Father J. V. Ducattillon.

Gabriela Mistral, that great South American soul, pleads for a better understanding between the great branches of Christianity, in the remarkable statement which she gave me:

"I am a Christian who twenty years ago hungered for that unity which labored the soul of Cardinal Mercier. I do not know

[61] *Ibid.*, pp. 175, 210.
[62] *Devant la Crise Mondiale.* Ed. de la Maison Française, New York, 1942.

upon whose shoulders may have fallen the mantle of pain and hope which that sainted man carried with such dignity. I cannot believe that that most transcendental apostleship, the constant search for that which will strengthen the bonds of fellowship within the Christian family, has been abandoned. The Church cannot relinquish, nor do I believe that she has, her hopes and efforts for the reconciliation of the Christian communities, especially in this apocalyptic time of war. She was always the enemy of chaos, and it is possible that Chaos, the mold in which our present world was cast, began to take shape when the great schism was completed, the worst of all divorces found on the pages of history. My friend, I think the heroic operation of the Christian soul to which we are all summoned is that of refusing to accept the finality of that unhappy event, or to consider it good, or useful, or inevitable, although much has been written and many events have occurred to persuade us that the damage is permanent and the loss irretrievable. I cannot believe in the eternity of evil, which would be hell itself. I prefer the mental agony of living in this long Purgatory of secession in which we find ourselves. For to me it seems to be Purgatory to have to live in a Christian community that has been spiritually slashed asunder. And I think we should bear it as an infinite humiliation and reckon it as one of our greatest acts of insanity, but never consider it a cosmic fatality doomed to last through eternity.

" You will understand now why I do not desire, not even for any benefit that might accrue to a believer, that the division between the two great interpretations of Christianity should be aggravated or that it should become embittered. To free our house (Latin America) of all Protestant missions would be a form of liberation which would predicate a species of Inquisition not created by us but whose dire consequences we would have to support. . . .

" For the present, we should aim at raising, however slightly it may be, the degree of tolerance which we now have, as Catholics and Protestants, in Spanish America. While we are able to greet each other as we walk our streets; while neither you nor we are compelled to live in ghettos, but are allowed to move freely in our countries; while we have dealings with one another and can gaze into each other's eyes unafraid, the holy fabric of Christian communion is torn but not destroyed. We would rend it to shreds were we to renew our belligerency. . . .

"Your social service activities benefit, not only the members of the foreign Protestant communities but also a large number of our own people, and large sections of the working classes, many of whom are not Protestant but atheistic. Your beneficence flows freely to all classes. . . .

"I am acquainted with the efficacy of several of your cultural activities, medical and agrarian. Some of them I consider superb. They are like the well of Samaria where a meeting took place whose significance equals one third of the Gospel.

"In such activities our hands may touch, and we may look at each other without bias, until on some great day we shall discover that we are one. The great reconciliation may spring from these fragments of fraternity. In the meantime, it is something that we do not believe each other to be Ormazd and Ahriman, and that we exchange greetings, and we share counsel and bestow help.

"For the present, then, let us not destroy the fellowship we already enjoy. This is the minimum of consideration that our spiritual nobility imposes upon us. On some other occasion I would like to talk with you about the major source of spiritual life, which, in our neglect, we have failed to see holds the magic formula for reunion: we shall talk, some day, my friend, about the Bible."

Protestant missions in Latin America must continue. Why? Because Jesus said, "Give ye them to eat." The physical hunger, want, and misery among the peons and Indians of Latin America are a challenge to Protestantism. But man cannot live by bread alone. There is spiritual hunger in the southland that only the Christian Gospel can satisfy. Hence Protestantism claims the privilege of placing the open Bible in the hands of its neighbors to the south. Jesus said, "Go, teach." Christian teaching is basic for the development of a Christian ethic and Christian character. Protestantism would follow its Master in this and continue being a teaching Church. The healing ministries of Jesus still challenge the Christian Church. " The healing of His seamless dress " is still by our beds of pain. Protestantism can do no other than follow the example of its Lord, and through its doctors and nurses minister to the wounded, stricken world. Protestantism must continue its missionary activities if it would make Christ regnant, not only in the life of others, but also in its own. Its prayer to Him who was the First Missionary is:

> " O Lord and Master of us all,
>   Whate'er our name or sign,
> We own Thy sway, we hear Thy call,
>   We test our lives by Thine."

Appendix A

I HAVE LIVED FOR MORE THAN TWENTY YEARS IN PERU, TEN IN ARGEN-
tina, six in Chile, and during brief periods in Uruguay, Bolivia,
Paraguay, Colombia, Panama, Ecuador, Brazil, and Cuba. I can
affirm that, with the honorable exception of a minority which is
authentically Catholic, the majority of so-called Latin American
Catholics place the trappings and externalities of religion above
its deeper and more intimate meaning. . . . Millions of Indians
and mestizos in the provinces, where for centuries the Catholic
Church has had no competition, have fallen into dead formulism
and a meaningless routine. They have missed the living doctrinal
content which is the root and substance of true Catholicism.

I feel that as a Catholic I must say these things. There are millions of Catholic men and women who, like me, are deeply preoccupied over this problem. . . . I was greatly comforted by
some of the aspects of North American Roman Catholicism. I was
impressed with the modern educational methods of the Sacred
Heart nuns of the convent school of Grand Coteau, La.[63] I spent
some marvelously peaceful days in that convent, occupying the
delightful guest room, the only man in an institution filled with
women! This is something that never could have occurred in
Latin America.

Hence it is important that representatives of North American
Catholicism should come to Latin America, bringing new life
with them, and an understanding liberalism; representatives who
would be permeable to new ideas and who would understand
human nature. But they should limit themselves to the field of
activities which is theirs. For now we are witnessing a " directed
religious policy " which requires that the abundant flow of American functionaries to South America should fulfill, if possible, the
prerequisite of being Roman Catholic.

We Latin Americans are inclined to be distrustful. We ask

[63] This is the school where Señor Seoane's sister, a nun, is teaching.

ourselves: "Why does a country which is predominantly Protestant send us delegations that are predominantly Catholic? Why does it try to hide its Protestantism?"

The labor groups in Latin America are also keenly aware of this problem. At a recent convention of the Chilean Confederation of Workers, which controls 500,000 members, three American delegates came from the United States. They were all Catholics. Consternation was created when these delegates visited a small Roman Catholic labor organization and were reported to have said, "Catholic workingmen must prepare to take under their control the direction of the labor movement." This declaration alarmed the Chilean labor delegates. They are determined not to allow clerical influences to penetrate their organization.

This attitude of favoring everything that is Roman Catholic has gone to the extreme of making it difficult for Protestant missionaries to travel to South America. This is a very serious matter. Among us freedom of religion is established by our constitutions and it offends us to think that an inquisitorial office has been established in some passport department which decides to whom we are to extend our hospitality! We want the best North Americans to come to our shores, be they Catholic or Protestant. The only requirement is that they should come with an authentic spirit of good neighborliness, desirous of fostering a progressive understanding and friendship between these two portions of the New World.

Protestant missions have carried out a quiet and tenacious effort of social service which compels our grateful recognition. Once when I was traveling in the Puno Mountain region of Peru where the Indians live in straw huts and under the most miserable and promiscuous conditions, I came upon a group of modest little houses, neatly painted, with ample windows for light and air, and a comfortable interior arrangement. They were built by Indians who had been evangelized and educated by Methodist missionaries who had gone to live among them in fulfilment of the Christian duty of helping one's fellow men. In Santiago, Chile, and in Buenos Aires, I have seen the effective work of the Salvation Army, which rescues the humbler classes from the influence of drink and which gives shelter to the homeless. These efforts have reacted on the Catholic circles, awakening them from their indifference and compelling them to undertake similar social activities.

That is why it would be an inexcusable mistake to revive the Inquisition in the matter of granting passports. It would, besides, work untold damage to the Catholic Church itself by granting her a monopoly which is contrary to the nature of things and opposed to the religious needs of Latin America.

Paradoxical as it may sound, we need both Catholic priests and Protestant pastors. That will lead to an improvement in our religious life. It will provide us with the opportunity for comparison such as St. Augustine had before he finally chose the road he was to follow. What we want is to see something accomplished in the realm of the spirit, something more democratic and just, that would strengthen our moral life; something free from dead routine and a deadlier intransigence; something humanely religious which will co-operate with us in our fight against sensuality and ignorance, against selfishness and wickedness. That is: we demand a work of the spirit that will vivify in our midst the creative forces of Christianity.

— *Manuel Seoane, Peruvian lawyer and author; Roman Catholic; at present editor of* Ercilla, *one of the most widely circulated weeklies of Chile.*

Appendix B

I am amazed at the question of whether the work of the Evangelical Church in Latin America is an obstacle to the Good Neighbor policy. Could we possibly consider the exchange of books, the intensification of radio programs, the visits of doctors, professors, and writers and the presence of lecturers and teachers from universities of other countries of America an obstacle to inter-American spiritual co-operation? Could cultural missions now be an obstacle in the way of the friendly relations which ought to result from the policy of Good Neighborliness? Is not this an absurdity?

As an Argentine I can reply to this question by recalling the historical experience of my country. When in 1853 the Constitutional Assembly met to draw up the Constitution by which we are governed, one of the fundamental questions to be faced was the following: whether to ratify a fundamental charter with the aim of assuring, maintaining, and perpetuating a religious uniformity in the population, even though this might mean a limitation of the number of inhabitants, or whether to fight against poverty, backwardness, and anarchy by adopting the policy of the open door and allowing the free influx of men and things and ideas. Our Constitution was therefore sanctioned on the following line . . . "to assure the benefits of liberty, for ourselves, for our descendants, and for all men everywhere who desire to live on Argentine soil."

Under the protection of this philosophy and these ideals, men of all nationalities and creeds came to our country, in the knowledge that they were protected by a liberal policy founded in religious freedom and sentiments of tolerance and mutual understanding.

For a good many years, therefore, we Argentines have understood what religious freedom meant to our material and mental progress. The Declaration of May, 1825, clearly stated the principles of our historical evolution. And in the pact of friendship signed during those same years with Great Britain, religious freedom for the English-speaking people was recognized.

For Argentines, therefore, religious freedom is a living element in our history, and the expression of a fundamental requirement in our final evolution. It has benefited us historically and been a strong factor in our civilization.

The work accomplished by English and American missionaries has caused no disturbance nor stirred up any incidents. The variety of their work — preaching, social service, educational recreation, solidarity with one's fellowman, — is looked upon with sympathy by those of us who would like to see the social aspects of religion reunite men. As an educator, I cannot forget the contribution which a Protestant made to the development of educa-

tion in my country when he introduced the Lancasterian method
of teaching.

On the other hand, the question which is under debate is really
an anachronism. Is not the world fighting even now for religious
liberty? Has not the whole world been horrorized by the consequences of religious totalitarianism?

The world of today and the world of tomorrow will need tolerance and liberty of conscience. These are moral and practical
necessities, because what system of doctrine can consider itself
the sole and exclusive possessor of truth in all its variety?

Unity in the midst of rich variety, presided over by liberty,
is the aim of democracy and humanity. And it is as necessary to
the latter as basal metabolism is to the physical life of the individual.

We must allow the variety of human soils to produce their
varied fruitage according to the nature of their beliefs!

The jealousies generated in the stuffy atmosphere of the sacristies should not be allowed to blind our vision of the way!

It is to be hoped that an understanding of the social evolution
of America may help those exceedingly zealous persons who
cause divisions, to understand also that a common root links
Catholics and Protestants: The Bible. In the presence of that
book jealousies and attitudes of intolerance ought to fade away.

And I say this further. For many South Americans the attitude
of the United States in strengthening the political power of the
Catholic Church in South America, especially in those countries
in which that Church adheres to the autocratic forms of government, is viewed with alarm. The final result is the strengthening
of dictatorship on our continent.

I am not hostile towards Catholicism. But it is necessary to emphasize that in Latin America there is a predominance of a clergy
which has been educated in the Hispanic and Roman tradition
whose spirit differs so fundamentally from that of militant Catholicism in other parts.

North American public opinion must understand that the Good
Neighbor policy means concretely that the Atlantic Charter must

also hold good for these parts of the world where there is much official talk of democracy and liberty but where people still live in subjugation.

— *Américo Ghioldi, member of the Argentine Congress; newspaper editor and educator.*

Appendix C

In no way do evangelical missions constitute an obstacle to the Good Neighbor Policy. A Catholic mission would hardly be able to do the truly democratic and spiritual work which is done by the Protestant pastors and missionaries. Uruguay is a country that is free from control by the clergy and in which there is absolute freedom of religion. The Constitution of 1917 abolished the privileges which the Catholic Church once enjoyed over other religions and since then the official statement of our Constitution is that the state favors no one religion, but protects them all.

The philosophic thought of this country is liberal. One can declare categorically that this is a country in which respect for all religions, even those which we do not practice, has itself become a religion.

Our public schools are lay schools because the state is free from control by the clergy.

The presence of Protestant missionaries in Uruguay has created a more favorable attitude toward the United States and brought about a better understanding between Uruguay and that country. Why? Protestant missionaries understand better than the Catholic missionaries the principles that are in line with the fundamental democratic spirit of the Uruguayan people. The evangelical missionaries have a profound sense of the ethical and social teachings of the New Testament. They adopt a much more sympathetic attitude toward the oppressed. This country is thoroughly committed to the idea of social justice. We are natural collaborators with those who preach social justice as an important part of their religious work.

National unity will not be destroyed by the entrance of creeds and philosophies different from those of the Catholic Church. One must not confuse unity with uniformity.

Catholic representatives who might come from the United States would hardly be able to represent the United States which Uruguay respects and loves. Because these missionaries from the North American Catholic clergy would represent a religious organization of totalitarian character. The Catholicism that we have known has always denied the freedom of religion which President Roosevelt himself proclaimed and which presupposes not only the right to worship God according to one's conscience, but the right to publicly declare the convictions that one holds.

The influence of Catholic intolerance reflected in the foreign policy of the United States is considered by people of liberal spirit in this country as a dangerous symptom of the totalitarian leanings of the United States. Therefore, there is a feeling of resentment among liberal sections of Uruguayan public opinion because of this surprising aspect of American policy. The problem is world-wide. Marshal Pétain, influenced by the worst Catholic elements in France, repudiated the democratic principles of the French Revolution. Admiral Leahy, and later Mr. Murphy, seemed able to accommodate themselves very easily to this attitude which means at the same time a repudiation of the Bill of Rights of the United States. This anti-American policy which the representatives of the United States look upon with indifference if not approval, affects the fundamental ethics of inter-American relations. The influence of Ambassador Hayes (a Catholic) in Spain has always been in the direction of favoring the totalitarianism of Franco. It is believed that the special representative to the Vatican, Mr. Taylor, has helped in determining all the subsequent policy in North Africa and in Italy. Similar examples could be given with respect to Czecho-Slovakia, Hungary, etc.

I have lived for two years in the United States and I hold a deep affection for its people. The foundation of democracy in that country is the small community of Puritan tradition. Evidently there is a clerical revolution underway in the world to destroy the gains which up to the present have been made for democracy. This is especially dangerous in the United States. I have heard complaints that the Government of the United States often sends people to these republics who are Roman Catholics and who are inclined with a sectarian spirit to favor everything that is Catholic. Unfortunately, this brings to life again among us a problem which we had thought was solved once for all; at least as far as Uruguay was concerned.

— *Hugo Fernandez Artucio, lawyer, author, and member of the Uruguayan Legislature.*

Appendix D

I was born in a country (Argentina) that practices freedom of worship, because it is a country made up of a population of immigrant origin. I have been nurtured in the liberal ideas which through the influence of John B. Alberdi were incorporated in our political Constitution. Thus our land could " appeal to all men everywhere who desire to live on Argentine soil." Consequently I cannot help but be in favor of religious tolerance. Besides this we need men whose lives are organized around a certain type of faith and whose morality would spring from that faith. This is very important, as I see it, and much more beneficial than a flow of individuals to our country with no faith at all. They could offer us no moral security for the future.

Freedom must be interpreted in the broadest possible way. It must be understood as the autonomy of the conscience and as carrying with it the right of propaganda. Liberty is not an accident in the Christian life but rather its essential condition, it is the *sine qua non* of Christianity. Without freedom we cannot live out our doctrine, we cannot even understand it. Liberty is so fundamental that I insist that it is also the right of those who do not believe as we do. We should not deprive others of that which we would not want them to deprive us. In the measure to which we respect the freedom of others, ours will be preserved.

For the sake of achieving national unity it is not necessary to exclude the representatives of non-Catholic faiths. For if other religious faiths were a menace to our personality, we should have to confess that our national unity was a very tenuous affair. If our spiritual cohesion is solid and sure, our national unity and solidarity will be able to meet the challenge of other currents of thought. Besides this, I do not believe that the different branches of Christianity within a Catholic country should be considered enemies, because if that country is really Catholic, it will be characterized by a Christian universality.

The presence of Protestant missionaries and teachers is not an obstacle to the Good Neighbor policy. I maintain that the work of these missionaries is a form — the most effective form — of that same policy. I would even venture to say that it is a form of solidarity in the spiritual realm. It is a practical Pan-Americanism! For within the family of America there should be no suspicions or misgivings, no offensive distinctions nor exclusions. The day in which America blots out the last frontiers — physical and economic — and suppresses all "spiritual tariff walls" we shall have realized the dream of a new world, and we shall have fulfilled the hopes that the old world built on those dreams.

— *Alberto Casal Castel, Argentine educator and university professor; distinguished Roman Catholic author and journalist.*

Appendix E

The presence of Protestant missionaries is not and cannot possibly be an offense to the people of Argentina in whose history, institutions and daily life freedom of conscience and of religious practice has always been held as something very precious. Eminent Catholics have made their contribution to this tradition.

Protestantism or the Reformation has made an indisputable moral contribution to the spiritual life of our America. We would be poorer today if to our shores had not come representatives of British, Swiss, French, Dutch and North American Protestant churches. In this as in all other relations competition revives and purifies.

Some years ago when I was the Envoy Extraordinary and Minister Plenipotentiary to Peru, I followed the advice of some Peruvian friends, who were not Protestant, and placed my two sons in the Protestant Anglo-Peruvian school of Lima which was under the principalship of an outstanding Christian gentleman, a wise and loving authority on things Spanish and Peruvian and former professor of the San Marcos University, Dr. John A. Mackay, whom, since that day I have been privileged to count among my dearest friends. In that school, housed in a very modest building with no chapel or church adjacent, my sons fell under Christian influences which molded their character and shaped their personality without awakening in them any spirit of sectarianism or intolerance. Dr. Mackay enjoyed the highest esteem of conspicuous Peruvian Catholics such as Javier Prado y Ugarteche, Victor Andrés Belaunde, José Matías Mansanilla, Carlos Ledgard, Luis Fernan Cisneros, Cristóbal Lozada y Puga and many others. My daughter attended a Catholic school in Chorrillos.

Great Britain has sent many and excellent persons and institutions to the Argentine Republic but her best gift during the last fifty years was the apostolic personality of William C. Morris, the most Argentine, the most sacrificial and the most spiritually fruitful foreigner that I have ever known.

In spite of the fanatical opposition of certain religionists, Morris, "that English Protestant curate," as they despisingly called him, carried on his great work patiently crowning it ever with a halo of tolerance, justice and love. He never asked any child who came to his schools or any teacher he employed, what their church affiliations were, but rather what their attitude was toward life and what their convictions were regarding life.

I knew this great man and loved and admired him as did also Catholics like Tancredo, Enrique and Humberto Pietranera, Lucio Correa Morales, Federico Pinedo (Senior), Angel Gallardo, etc. When as a very poor young man I was starting out in life, I offered to help Morris in his educational work by giving free classes in Argentine history and civics. This was my first job as a teacher and I held it for three years. I am proud to recall this beginning of a friendship which lasted for more than forty years.

The United States has been to us a model in the matter of child-welfare. No country has expressed its sense of responsibility for the care of its children so eloquently in wise legislation as the United States. No people have been so deeply Christian in their attention to the moral and physical health and needs of their children as the people who inhabit the land of Washington, Lincoln and Horace Mann. It is from that people that we have received our example and our stimulus and they have shown us the way.

I have visited nearly all the Salesian missions in the country, especially in the remote regions of southern Patagonia and I never found that the courageous disciples of Don Bosco had ever had any difficulty with or been molested by the pastors, missionaries or preachers of the evangelical faith.

— *Antonio Sagarna, member of the Supreme Court of Argentina.*

Appendix F

One symptom that serious changes are taking place in the world is the fact that the religious question has again come to the front. During the closing years of the last century and the first thirty years of our present century, at least in Latin America, no layman who respected himself, would have shown any interest in this question. He would have been ashamed to do so; such interest would have proved him an inferior type of man. But not today. Governments have lost no time. Realizing that religion is capable of regaining its powers and privileges they have laid hold of it for the purpose of bending it to their will and making it serve their purposes. And it is indispensable that we study this new fact now while there is time and opportunity so that when the days of adjustment come, we may not find ourselves the victims of one more serious error, an error which would spell tremendous failure for our spirituality, the anxious spirituality of our America.

In the United States a policy of " temporal " captivation is being followed with the aid of the " eternal " interests of the Church. North American officials who discuss the matter of the influence of Protestant and Catholic missions, who argue as to the advisability of weakening the former and strengthening the latter, for the simple reason that it is *expedient* for their supposed *political* interests, fall into the most vulgar of perversions and the most absurd of all errors. Missionaries or ecclesiastical agencies that lend their support, for *spiritual* reasons, to the *temporal* purposes of their government, place religion at the beck and call of politics and expose it to the consequences of politics. In so doing they are traitors to their mission, their mandate and their vows. They are perjurers and simoniacal.

We Latin Americans will always be suspicious of those who come to us clothed in extraordinary powers and privileges which we interpret as revealing some definite, ulterior purpose. No Latin American will accept with sincerity religious missions that are supported by regimented "priorities" of the State Department. To our creole spirit of distrust, a factor which is not reckoned with by Washington's political strategists, every missionary "made in U.S.A." is looked upon as an insurance agent, or a banker who wishes to place a loan, or an employee of the Coordinator of Inter-American Relations, or a member of the F.B.I. If what Washington officials want is to discredit religion *per se*, they have already made some progress. Let it be clear: everything that comes to us stamped with an official *made in U.S.A.* seal suggests self-interest or some ulterior purpose. Implicitly it links itself with the dollar sign. It is worth so much; it is an object of barter. It can be of use. I know that there are many things — and ideas — in the United States, that represent high value in themselves. But you cannot expect those who have known only the overwhelming material power of the United States to believe that those other values exist. Yesterday, in an economy of peace, they knew the United States through her capitalistic enterprises established with full autonomy and a management independent of the countries in which it functioned. Today, in a war period, they see her through trade organizations eager to be ahead in any deal. Religious propaganda regimented from Washington will lead to a weakening of religious ties and, soon or late, will be considered an ally of imperial penetration. Then it will be that Christianity will end up by appearing to be an expression of imperialism. For the good of all concerned, it were well to avoid this confusion. The days that are ahead will bring us much pain. Men should be able to find somewhere a firm wall against which to lean their weary, sweaty heads. And that support must continue to come from Christianity.

Furthermore, there could be no error more grievous or more unbrotherly than that of thinking that, as far as Christianity is concerned, we are on the same level as the Africans and Asiatics. That is, to consider us as "infidels" or "pagans." They who so think forget that in relation to Christianity we do not need colonizers; we have moved ahead; we could do some colonizing on our account. It hurts our religious consciousness and our civilized self-respect that any one should pretend to teach us as they would the natives of Mozambique or Tibet what the Christian religion is and even more so, when they pretend to teach us what Catholicism is. We have experts in these subjects who could do honor to a university course in the United States. The organization of a systematic Catholic crusade in the United States to work upon Latin America is equivalent to our launching a movement to Protestantize the United States. So much for the fundamental aspect of this problem. As regards the form under which it presents itself, let me say that a mission for the propagation of the faith will be self-defeating, if it comes to us subsidized or favored by the government whose fraternal motives are not quite clear and whose past reveals very patently its inclination toward domination and absorption. That kind of religious approach carries with it suicidal germs. And what is worse, it may weaken profoundly the simple faith of the common people. This is a tragic price to pay for some small victories won in the upper sphere of society. This in itself would be a serious loss for high religion. To strengthen the Church in its higher social relations at the expense of the faith of the common man, is equivalent to the destruction of one of the pillars of Christianity.

I am not forgetting the difference between the spirit of North American Catholicism and that of Hispanic-American Catholicism. Arguing from that fact one can make a strong case in favor of an active interchange between the two groups. But "active" does not mean "official," and in this day of global war we know that all traffic is official, or at least with official sympathy back of it. Consequently when large groups of Catholic propagandists come with official approval from a predominantly capitalist and Protestant country to countries that are still semi-colonial and Catholic, that movement appears as a menace and is far from being characterized by the spirit of fair play. We sense in it some unworthy motive which has not been kept hidden very successfully.

One of the arguments which one sometimes hears in connection with this problem is " that the spiritual unity of Latin America " must be preserved and strengthened on the basis of religious unity. The force of the argument is apparent only. It reflects the same fallacy as that other phrase: " Our unity of tradition." Those who use this phrase seem to think that " unity of tradition " should include all the characterizations of the colonial regime of Philip II: oligarchy, absolutism, intolerance and racism. But they forget that the greater part of our colonial history is the story of the struggle of the townhall popular assembly against the government, the struggle of submerged groups through local and racial insurrections. They forget that nearly all the history of our period of independence develops under the inspiration of the cult of free thought. All the political founders of our independence were free thinkers as were also the majority of the intellectual leaders of that period.

As a matter of fact, if there is one thing that we lack it is an affirmative spiritual unity. Having grown up in a dogmatic atmosphere which has bred in us the habit of closed affirmations and final negations, we lack that inner fire which reveals the presence of a true faith. Faith and dogma have never been synonymous. The former is life itself; the latter is its crystallization. Between the two, history develops. Faith is tireless and creative; dogma is finally static. We, in Latin America, are united in our scepticism and negation, because we have always lived under the sign of monopoly: economic during the colonial period, political during the earlier independence period, financial later on and clerical all the time. Our Catholics, who constitute the immense majority on our continent, are poor at the practice of their beliefs because they lack that inner fire which is the result of a deep and sincere faith.

This element of faith is absent because our people never discuss their spiritual problems; they are told what to believe; they never elaborate or work out their beliefs. That is why contact with other creeds could serve as a stimulus to a real faith. Why is it that Catholics in the United States have a higher and more constructive sense of their religion and of life? For the reason that they live face to face with a vigorous and watchful Protestant Church. Why is it that Protestants in Latin America are nearly always exemplary? Because they live under the shadow of a powerful Catholic Church.

I am not forgetting that from the standpoint of philosophy and religion, there is only one Truth and he who claims to possess it will not admit that some one else has a part of it. But this assurance of monopoly, were it possible, should not rule out an attitude of tolerance that would at least attribute sincerity to him who has accepted a different creed and who believes that he and he alone has the Truth. To see honorable intentions only in one's fellow-believers is surely the acme of sectarianism and the antithesis of that marvelous spirit of fraternity and tolerance exemplified by the Nazarene. The serious aspect of this problem is that it represents one of the weaknesses of the Latin American religious spirit.

Catholicism in Spain developed under conditions very different from that of other countries, including France and England. The struggle against the Moors lasted for 800 years and it was bitter and bloody. And, as always happens in any long controversy or struggle, each side took on some definite characteristics. The Spanish church became aggressive, pugnacious and intolerant as was natural in the struggle against the intolerance and warlikeness of Mahomet. The Spanish church came to America where it found nothing to fight except the superstitions of the indigenous peoples. Nevertheless, it did not lose its anti-Moorish crusading quality. When the present Spanish and Spanish-American church is compared with its sister organizations in France, Italy, Germany and the Anglo-Saxon countries, one discovers that it has some very distinctive features. The very activities of the Jesuit order, so frequently combated in colonial South America as well as in the later republican period, may be better understood if one remembers that the founder of that religious order had two well defined qualities: he was a soldier and he was a Spaniard. But we South Americans are characterized fundamentally by a "mixed race" mentality; we are part Indian and part Iberian. Our culture came to us from the Mediterranean, from Frenchmen and Italians and is consequently predominantly sceptical. In order to find itself, our spiritual unity needs to feel the challenge of thoughts and attitudes that will be different from ours, thoughts and attitudes that will be the outcome of a powerful inner force. So shall we learn how to argue without aggression, how to compare without producing schism, how to go deeply into things without digging graves. The root of our one-sidedness must be dug up. The selfish sources of monopoly must be dried up, and the springs of tolerance and free discussion deepened.

It used to be said frequently that immigration would destroy the essence of the spirit of America. But today we know that, on the contrary, it strengthened it. Once it was said that Spain was a retrograde influence grafted on our life. But today we know that she mingles well with our blood. The Indian was proscribed and considered altogether barbarous, but now we know that he has greatly helped our personality to find itself. The same mingling goes on with cultural ingredients and occurs in the field of religious ideas. We live in Latin America under the powerful suggestion of distant horizons rather than near prison walls. Fundamentally a believing people though temporarily sceptical and consequently filled with uncertainty, Latin Americans need to find their way by looking up, by taking their bearings and examining different routes. My own experience has taught me that this slow and painful method, this wading through layers of patient routine, is the best way of getting at the essence of things. Let people from everywhere come to our countries; let them come each with his truth, his culture, his language, his religion. Here, with us, they will be converted to what is ours in the measure to which what is ours is purified and amplified in contact with what is theirs. Our great weakness, I repeat, is that of living colonially and of being treated as colonials. We do not need liberators whose first word to us would be one learned in some foreign government office, however generous or righteous that word might be. Let religious faith come to us without the trappings of monopoly and without the rubrications of imperial privilege. Faith is not created nor strengthened by external methods. It is an intimate process, an unsettling process, an eminently personal process. It is generated as the result of an irresistible necessity and it develops best in open spaces, in contact with other lives, other ideas and above all in contact with nature which though close to man is still so foreign to man.

Let no government office, therefore, pretend to take us under its tutelage even in matters religious. Let them leave us free to determine at least our own metaphysical destiny, since they have deprived us of the privilege of doing this with our material existence. And may they believe us when we say that there are areas in individual and collective life where the worst prescription . . . is a prescription! And the problem we have been considering is a case in point.

— *Luis Alberto Sánchez, lawyer, author, and lecturer.*

Appendix G

I have complete respect for the Catholic dogma. I am passionately enamoured of Christ's standard of morals. I do not wish to enter into dogmatic problems for which my preparation is insufficient. I respect the opinions of the Catholic church and I try to confine the expression of my own opinion to those points which I see with absolute clarity and which guide my conscience. This fact should be borne in mind to understand my position and why I attempt to deal with these questions from the social point of view.

In Spain, the situation of the Catholics is the following: A small minority, mystically inclined, illumined and convinced, profess the Catholic religion with absolute sincerity, purity and blind faith. They deserve the highest respect, because, whether or not they be people of strong intellect, they are without doubt, pure in heart. Another group loves and follows the doctrines of Christ without thought of Catholicism or the Gospel. They guide their lives by the marvelous moral principles that come to them from Calvary. Still another and larger group is composed of those who exploit their religion for their own benefit. They invoke it and pay lip service to it in order to protect their interests, their vanity and their comfort. The immense majority of the Spanish people, particularly the humble classes which are totally indifferent, do not wish to have anything to do with God or His church and do not profess any positive religion. This may seem a harsh statement, but please remember that learned prelates and priests have spoken of the falling away of the masses from religion. That this is true is proved by a recent example. The so-called Catholics are the ones responsible for the war in Spain. They called themselves patriots and welcomed the invasion of their country by foreign troops. They called themselves believers in the law of God and yet coldly executed their brothers during the five years after victory, and many hundreds of them have been imprisoned. They are the self-styled continuers of Spanish history, and yet everything they do is in contradiction to the honoured traditions of Spain. The clergy has lavished attacks against the legitimate regime of the country, with the exception of the Basque priests and those fifty odd priests who were photographed in the Carmona jail surrounding the layman Julian Besteiro, an unbelieving socialist but a good man and virtuous.

Therefore you will realize that in Spain Catholicism is going through a great crisis, the outcome of which it is impossible to predict. If the Catholics were humble, virtuous, poor and just and contributed with an intelligent effort to social reform, Catholicism in Spain would reach a glorious culmination. As they are all the contrary, Spanish Catholicism has fallen to the dust.

With regard to Catholicism in Argentina, my position as a guest makes it difficult for me to express myself. But I am afraid that conditions are similar to those in Spain. The fact that all the fascists here are Catholics and that they fight liberty and democracy, is a clear indication that they are mainly defenders of privilege rather than convinced followers of a religious faith. Add to this the disconcerting opulence of religious ceremonial, the wealth with which images are adorned, the pomp and magnificence displayed by the Bishops, the luxury with which they surround themselves, the enthusiastic support which the wealthy give the Church and you will understand the aversion of the working and humbler classes for religion. But please note that I do not attribute these defects only to Spain and Argentina, but also to the other countries where Catholics act in the same manner. In other words, if Catholicism turns entirely to Christ, it will attain a glorious resurrection, but if it persists in remaining apart from Christ, it will be condemned to ruin.

On the question as to whether the Protestant Church has a mission to fulfill in Latin America, we are liable to differ. As I respect entirely the dogma and organization of the Catholic Church, I think that the Protestants have nothing to gain here or anywhere else. But as you are a Protestant, you have the right to think that you are free to preach your doctrines wherever you like. That is to say, from a religious standpoint our two questions are irreconcilable; but from the standpoint of civil rights, I who am a sincere liberal must respect liberty of worship, preaching and propaganda. Naturally, it is only right that I should wish you to fail in your efforts; but legally I must not allow anybody to stop you.

You ask me whether Protestants meddle in politics? The answer is simple: Protestants as individuals do intervene in politics, but the Protestant churches as an organization do not. This is the main point of difference between the Catholic Church and the Protestant Church. The Catholic Church has always been in politics. The Popes have had temporal power, have celebrated alliances and treaties, have waged wars, and for this reason have been exposed to the accidents of political fortune which history records. The Bishops have dealings with the Governments, intervene in the elections, present their own candidates, etc. When in Spain the elections of February, 1936, were held, in which the Popular Front triumphed, the Bishop of Barcelona ordered the Host to be exposed in all the Churches so as to guarantee the victory of the Rightists. Can you conceive of any greater folly? To everyone's

amusement the Leftists won, and the joke that circulated for days
was that the Host had lost the election.

The fact that the Church should have a definite political bias
appears to me to be one of the deepest mistakes on her part. Every
Catholic can and should take part in whatever political movements please him and face the results. But the Church as such has
no reason for mixing in these conflicts between men. It should
give unto Caesar what is Caesar's. Protestantism has been wise
in following the opposite course. Its members engage in whatever
political action they please but their churches, as institutions, do
not interfere in politics at all. Catholicism would have avoided
many mistakes, many dangers and many errors if it had kept to
its mission of seeking and saving lost souls. Allow me to elaborate:
The church may have a political *opinion* or *outlook* on questions
related to God, but what it may never engage in is political action.

Regarding your question: Is Latin America so completely Catholic or Christian that it does not need Protestant influence, I shall
deny the presupposition that is back of this question. All the
Latin American and European countries profess adherence to
Catholicism but are not Catholic. Of every one hundred people
who go to church there is probably not one who follows the com-
mandments of God. In addition the work of the Protestants meets
with a grave difficulty, which is the multiplicity of its sects,
churches and beliefs. The great force of the Catholic Church (and
one of the elements which lends strength to the belief in its divine
origin) is its unity. From this it draws a firmness, an assurance of
progress, an orderly development, which cannot exist where the
churches are divided. You will always have to face this great obstacle and it arises out of some of your fundamental doctrines
which seem wrong to me. But we must not enter further into this
as it would lead me into territory which I am anxious to avoid.

The presence of Protestant missionaries is not an obstacle to
the harmonious relations between North and South America?

Such relationships are economic, political and civil in nature.
And it is other factors, not the religious aspects, which have any
influence on such a relationship. The Protestants in no way complicate the problem. The Jews are much more numerous than the

Protestants, and nobody would be so stupid as to say that the Jewish groups constitute an obstacle between the two civilizations. Whether the relations are good or bad depends on other concepts and other causes. At present there is an evident tenseness in the relations between the United States and Argentina for motives which each interprets differently. But nobody would claim that if many Protestants were to come here things would improve or get worse, nor that the same would happen were the ones who are here asked to leave. The legislature of both countries established liberty of worship in full knowledge of what they were doing. For this reason, neither are the Catholics an obstruction in the North where the Protestants are in an immense majority, nor do the Protestants hinder in the South where the majority are Catholic.
— *Angel Ossorio y Gallardo, distinguished Spanish jurist and writer; Roman Catholic; ex-president of the Spanish Bar Association and former Ambassador of the Spanish Republic to Argentina.*

Appendix H

QUES.: Do you believe that Protestant missions in Spanish America ought to be sacrificed on the altar of the Good Neighbor policy?

ANS.: Neither as a gesture of good will nor from a desire to improve on former policies, do I believe that that policy should try to alter any human principle which is fundamental in our countries.

Freedom for all creeds is one of the distinguishing republican honors of South America. The laws which establish that freedom are a guarantee, first of all, for the Catholics, then for the Protestants, and also for the Orthodox Church and the Jews. Tampering with that pillar of bronze, which is our religious liberty, hammered out for us on a thrice heated forge, or mutilating the struggling roots of the spirit of freedom, seems an adventure fraught with danger, and I always fear such ventures on the part of young and inexperienced peoples. Such enterprises stir up, first of all, curious fancies, then release dark passions and finally lend strength to evil instincts.

I am not forgetting the position of Catholicism in Latin America. It is the highest in the plane of our moral institutions. Numerically her strength is overwhelming and by her side others are like weak reeds or tender saplings. Lords and masters well established in their broad moral domains, the Catholicisms of the south, and the Chilean leading them all, permitted themselves the luxury of being generous, — a grace always elegant, and they consented to live together with other creeds and sects. The laws that separate Church and State, accepted in Chile by the *sagesse* of a prince of the Church who was also princely in his wisdom, Msgr. Errázuriz, do not signify the surrender of the Catholic conscience to the State. Some of us believe they mean something very different. We believe they signify a degree of liberation that leads to greater ease and comfort. Nearly all States tend to overwhelm the representatives of spiritual values, belittling them with a protection that carries with it the suspicion of some deal or barter.

On the other hand, the proposition that Protestantism should be sacrificed could turn out to be a Trojan horse to Catholicism. To begin with, as far as I know, it has not been suggested by South American Roman Catholicism.

Supposing that Protestant missions and their social service activities could be suppressed, either rapidly or gradually, I fear that, little by little, an atmosphere of resentment and finally of hatred for Catholicism would be engendered.

I am filled with doubt and even fear at the thought of a Catholic domination based on eliminations or on restrictions double-dyed in privilege. Creeds, just as with strong government regimes, do not need the support of favor or privilege. And if they seek such favors or accept them, they fall into great temptation.

QUES.: Do you think that we should hope and work for the ultimate reunion of all Christian groups?

ANS.: I am a Christian who twenty years ago hungered for that unity which labored the soul of Cardinal Mercier. I do not know upon whose shoulders may have fallen the mantle of pain and hope which that sainted man carried with such dignity. I cannot believe that that most transcendental apostleship, the constant search for that which will strengthen the bonds of fellowship within the Christian family, has been abandoned. The Church cannot relinquish, nor do I believe that she has, her hopes and efforts for the reconciliation of the Christian communities, especially in this apocalyptic time of war. She was always the enemy of chaos, and it is possible that Chaos, the mold in which our present world was cast, began to take shape when the great schism was completed, the worst of all divorces found on the pages of history. My friend, I think the heroic operation of the Christian soul to which we are all summoned is that of refusing to accept the finality of that unhappy event, or to consider it good, or useful, or inevitable, although much has been written and many events have occurred to persuade us that the damage is permanent and the loss irretrievable. I cannot believe in the eternity of evil, which would be hell itself. I prefer the mental agony of living in this long Purgatory of secession in which we find ourselves. For to me it seems to be Purgatory to have to live in a Christian community that has been spiritually slashed asunder. And I think we should bear it as an infinite humiliation and reckon it as one of our greatest acts of insanity, but never consider it a cosmic fatality doomed to last through eternity.

You will understand now why I do not desire, not even for any benefit that might accrue to a believer, that the division between the two great interpretations of Christianity should be aggravated or that it should become embittered. To free our house (Latin America) of all Protestant missions would be a form of liberation which would predicate a species of Inquisition not created by us but whose dire consequences we would have to support.

QUES.: On what do you base your hopes of a reconciliation between the various branches of Christianity?

ANS.: Hopes that cry out in despair, are those which have no tomorrow. True hope is never characterized by improper haste (the haste of pride). The main scandal of Christendom is that we should live, and eat, and sleep in the midst of a guerilla warfare that fills us with no shame, that does not seem to sadden us with

its unnatural hatred and which even causes rejoicing in some
quarters. . . . The Scandal lies in the fact that we do not see with
the broad vision of our soul as well as that of our eyes, that we
are crucifying our Lord again and this time it is not done by Roman centurions nor by a Jewish mob, but by us, Christians.

I find no word in my tongue nor in any other that I know, strong
enough to condemn this sullen sin of stubbornness, whose fruitage
of death and dissolution is everywhere evident. It is suspended in
the air of Europe and Asia and America, like poisoned apples
that turn to ashes.

QUES.: But, since the schism of Christendom is so serious in its
origins, what means do you think are available for undoing the
evil or at least for keeping it from being aggravated?

ANS.: We women do not create great ideas nor organize great
deliverances. But sometimes we manage to complete the circle of
a marvellous fellowship, and we frequently manage to check internal strife of every kind.

For the present, we should aim at raising, however slightly it
may be, the degree of tolerance which we now have, as Catholics
and Protestants, in Spanish America. While we are able to greet
each other as we walk our streets; while neither you nor we are
compelled to live in ghettos, but are allowed to move freely in
our countries; while we have dealings with one another and can
gaze into each other's eyes unafraid, the holy fabric of Christian
communion is torn but not destroyed. We would rend it to shreds
were we to renew our belligerency.

QUES.: Are you at all acquainted with our missionary work
in these Latin countries?

ANS.: Yes, I have seen something of it and possibly the best.
I have witnessed some deeply stirring acts performed quietly and
without ostentation. In your great social work (agricultural
schools, clinics, cultural societies) Catholics sometimes co-operate
with Protestants, each with loyalty to his convictions, and while
this may not be more than a gesture of courtesy and propriety, we
must not despise these crumbs of approximation. Nothing is lost
while people preserve the golden thread of fellowship, and when
that thread vibrates the human heart feels life throb within it.

QUES.: What other reasons would you mention that justify the continuation of Protestant work in Spanish America?

ANS.: The primary reason, which should have been mentioned sooner, is that those activities fall within what the League of Nations calls the "rights of minorities." A careful census of Protestants in our midst would reveal an impressive total. To weaken or suppress their institutions would be in the nature of an odious illegality. It would lead to resentment and later to dangerous outbursts. It is outstandingly true that liberty alone conciliates, placates and calms.

We Iberian Catholics must remember that these Anglo-Saxon and South American Protestant groups need their churches, their services of worship, and their religious press just as much as they need the piece of ground on which they have built their homes, their factories and their playgrounds. They feed equally upon the food of our soil, the teaching of their religious books and the word of their missionaries. And this spiritual hunger seems to me to be more intense in them than in us. I have not seen our people carrying the Gospels in the minimum baggage allowed for a plane trip. I have seen your Protestant people do that. Life in these lands of ours, to be happy, must be complete. No Christian can consider life fulfilled, if it lacks the salt of high wisdom. Protestants are entitled to their share of spiritual teaching just as they receive their portion of grain and native fruits.

Your social service activities benefit, not only the members of the foreign Protestant communities but also a large number of our own people, and large sections of the working classes, many of whom are not Protestant but atheistic. Your beneficence flows freely to all classes.

I am acquainted with the efficacy of several of your cultural activities, medical and agrarian. Some of them I consider superb. They are like the well of Samaria where a meeting took place whose significance equals one third of the Gospel.

In such activities our hands may touch, and we may look at each other without bias, until on some great day we shall discover that we are one. The great reconciliation may spring from these fragments of fraternity. In the meantime, it is something that we do not believe each other to be Ormazd and Ahriman, and that we exchange greetings, and we share counsel and bestow help.

For the present, then, let us not destroy the fellowship we already enjoy. This is the minimum of consideration that our spiritual nobility imposes upon us. On some other occasion I would like to talk with you about the major source of spiritual life, which, in our neglect, we have failed to see holds the magic formula for reunion: we shall talk, some day, my friend, about the Bible.

— *Gabriela Mistral, Chilean poetess and writer.*

Appendix I

I was born into a Catholic family and was made to observe the religious precepts of that Church. And I have continued as an adherent of that Church, partly as a result of the force of tradition and sentimental reasons, and partly because of the need which we all have for spiritual food.

My later studies in philosophy, history, literature, together with my reading and my knowledge of life and of people gave me a broadening conception of religion. I continue to consider myself linked to the Catholic Church, which I attend from time to time. I hear and judge with my own reasoning the most authoritative spokesmen of the Church, especially when they are dealing with subjects relating to the social order, because I believe that in this day and age the teaching of Christ applied to personal life and to the life of the community is the only force capable of saving humanity. Contact with men and women of other branches of Christianity has given me the opportunity to appreciate the valuable influence of their work in the field of spiritual culture.

I have visited conventions of Methodist women; I have often listened to the preaching of Protestant pastors; I maintain a close friendship with the deaconess of the Protestant Church in my native town; in company with Catholic friends I have attended a spiritual retreat organized by members of other churches. In one of them I heard the inspired voice of Susanna Dietrich; I know the philanthropic work done by the great Mr. Morris, which is the admiration of all. I know of many schools and cultural centers which are doing a highly constructive piece of work and exerting a valuable Christian influence. All of this enables me to affirm with all sincerity that they constitute a moral and spiritual force of great importance for the development of our country.

Together with thousands of other Catholics I have listened with fervent respect to the messages of truth brought to us by such men as Dr. John R. Mott and Dr. George Howard. I believe that it is a privilege for us to be visited by these missionaries who lift our thought to new heights, who call us to the consideration of problems of transcendental importance, and who help us on toward perfection by the pathway that each may choose or may have chosen according to the dictates of his own conscience.

— *Doctora Angela Santa Cruz, distinguished Argentine educator.*

Appendix J

I shall answer your question [64] in the words of a Chaplain of King Albert of Belgium who visited our country in 1922. He said: "An appreciable percentage of the population is faithful to the Church and practices Catholicism. There is, on the other hand, a large number of indifferent and superstitious people. There is an insufficient number of priests to attend adequately to the indoctrination and guidance of the people. The priests that are available are too reduced in numbers to be able to attend to the religious needs of a country of such vast dimensions as Brazil."

Missionaries are in no way an obstacle to the Good Neighbor policy. They are making a most valuable contribution to the moral and cultural development of our country. They help us understand the United States better and they interpret certain aspects of the life of that country to us.

Protestantism has served as a stimulus to Roman Catholicism. It is a warning to that Church that it must awaken from the sleep of indifference into which it had been lulled as a result of its isolation from other currents of Christian thought. When Roman

[64] I had asked him, "How Roman Catholic is Brazil?"

Catholicism was our State religion and other religions were prohibited in Brazil, Catholicism entered a period of decay. The freedom which was later granted to other religions and the separation of Church and State, have been helpful to the Roman Church itself. It has been compelled to open more schools, create more parishes and dioceses and build more churches.

Protestantism has given Brazil upright and honest men who have been of great service to our country. It has awakened in its followers a sense of responsibility and developed in them a staunchness of character that has become a veritable national asset. It has stirred up in its people a hunger to know and given them a taste for reading. One of Brazil's greatest grammarians was a Protestant.

I give no weight to the fear that Protestant propaganda may weaken the political unity of our country. There are countries of solid national unity whose population professes a variety of creeds; Switzerland, Holland, Canada, Prussia and even France are examples. On the other hand there are many Catholic countries whose national unity is weak, as in Spain, torn by internal dissension; Italy, whose lack of national cohesion explains, in large part, its misfortunes; Central America, Catholic and divided into a number of small republics. There does not seem to be any necessary relation between national cohesion and the creed professed by the majority. And if there were, then the facts would favor the Protestant countries where a great and more perfect political unity exists. Incidentally, there is no doubt that in the present war Catholic countries reveal a notable weakness in their spirit of resistance and combativeness, due, no doubt, to their internal divergencies.

Protestantism is a democratic-federative movement. The Christian Protestant world is a vast federation of churches, governed democratically in conformity with the model laid down by the primitive church. The life of the local congregations is intense and greatly contributes to the incorporation of evangelical ideals into the life of the community. It tends to the creation of a people who themselves become priests and kings. The people themselves exercise the ministry of the altar.

Roman Catholicism, in its organization, follows the model of an

absolute monarchy with accentuated political activities. And be
it remembered: in the field of politics men will always be divided.
The doctrine of Christ, on the other hand, is a power which makes
for solidarity.

— *Manuel Carlos Ferraz, distinguished Brazilian jurist and President of the Appellate Court of Brazil.*

Appendix K

There is one aspect of the Good Neighbor policy which should
be taken into account and which is not often mentioned. The reality which may exist in this policy is hidden under layers of
honeyed sentimentalism. This is dangerous and might mean the
failure of the promise which this policy holds for the future relations of America. The attempt is made to hide two unpleasant
truths. First, that Latin Americans want to camouflage the hope
they have that the United States will continue to contribute generously, and with cold cash, to their urgent needs or caprices.
And secondly, the North Americans try to hide the fact that they
have substituted for the policy of the "big stick" that of a cultural
infiltration which is purposely slow but rigidly inflexible.

That the Good Neighbor policy may result in much good for the
united growth of the Americas, is not to be doubted; but that will
be on condition that problems caused by over-sentimentality and
hypocrisy be put aside and the facts faced frankly. One of these
facts is that the North American democracy is, by a great majority,
Protestant. Consequently we Latin Americans cannot expect that
the representatives which the United States might send us, in whatever field of culture, thought or business, should be carefully
chosen from among the Catholic minority in that country. Among
these agents of Good Neighborliness are the well-prepared, well-
educated Protestant missionaries, who have as much right to offer
their merchandise as the industrial missionaries who come from
the United States. I do not conceive that one can be a good neighbor if he begins by refusing to greet his fellow-man and by closing
the door of his house against him when he comes, with all cour-

tesy, to offer the trinkets or the jewels which he carries in his show case. Especially when the neighbor is an estimable person who lives in the big house to the north.

It does not seem to me that the governments of these republics should yield to the pressure being brought to bear by the Roman Catholic hierarchies for the purpose of obtaining a virtual monopoly in control over the souls of men. This converting of Latin America into a religious closed shop would only revive, in the age of bombing planes, the old fanaticism of the Inquisition, the Calvinists and the Puritans. Neither do I consider it desirable from a cultural standpoint, since every proclamation of a new doctrine, every new interpretation of dogmas or beliefs, are movements of the mind that lead to free examination, to reading, and to the awakening of the spirit. And it seems to me that one article that is urgently needed in this land, is the merchandise of ideas, whatever the wrapping in which they come. It is time that the breezes of the Reformation reached our lands. They have delayed too long. We need them to blow through some sections of our countries that still struggle along lines of the sixteenth century.

— *Enrique Uribe White, one of Colombia's distinguished intellectuals; director of the National Library of Bogotá, Colombia.*